Best of

SAIL
MAGAZINE'S

Things
That
Work

Best of *SAIL* MAGAZINE'S Things That Work

International Marine
Camden, Maine

International Marine/
Ragged Mountain Press

A Division of The **McGraw·Hill** *Companies*

10   9   8   7   6   5   4   3   2

Copyright © 1998 by International Marine, a division of The McGraw-Hill Companies.
All rights reserved. The publisher takes no responsibility for the use of any of the materials or
methods described in this book, nor for the products thereof. The name "International Marine"
and the International Marine logo are trademarks of The McGraw-Hill Companies. Printed in the United
States of America.

Library of Congress Cataloging-in-Publication Data
Best of SAIL magazine's things that work.
     p.   cm.
  Includes index.
  ISBN 0-07-058053-7
  1. Sailboats—Equipment and supplies.   2. Sailboats—Maintenance
and repair. I. Sail.
VM351.B46   1998
628.8'223dc21   97-48509
                                              CIP

Questions regarding the content of this book should be addressed to:

International Marine
P.O. Box 220
Camden, ME 04843

Questions regarding the ordering of this book should be addressed to:

The McGraw-Hill Companies
Customer Service Department
P.O. Box 547
Blacklick, OH 43004
Bookstores: 1-800-722-4726

The Best of SAIL Magazine's Things That Work is printed on 60-pound Renew Opaque Vellum, an acid-free paper
which contains 50 percent recycled water paper (preconsumer) and 10 percent postconsumer waste paper.

Printed by R.R. Donnelley, Harrisonburg, VA.
Edited by Herb and Nancy Payson and Erik Nelson; design (and cover design) by Robert H. Eckhardt;
editorial production by Allison Peter; all illustrations by Kim Downing except pages 103 and 183.

To sailors everywhere who work on their boats,
especially to those who have contributed ideas to
SAIL Magazine's "Things That Work" column—
this book is for you.

INTRODUCTION

Nancy and I have been fielding contributions for SAIL's Things That Work for four years now, and we've found that the tinkerers and putterers of the world comprise a group with a common interest that's almost as compelling as the bond among long-distance cruisers. It's a group of which both Nancy and I are happy to be members.

And if you think that fielding ideas from fellow sailors might pall after four years, think again. New ideas fascinate us, and the process of actively imagining each one step by step never ceases to tickle our brain cells. If an idea is so sketchy that I can't take it through my step-by-step process, I run it by Nancy. If neither of us understand, I figure most readers won't either. In some cases if the idea is good, we ask the author for a better description, illustration, or whatever is necessary for clarification. More often, if it hasn't run in an earlier column, a good idea will be published.

By the way, there's enough danger involved in editing to keep the most jaded adventurer alert. Several times, most often at boat shows, I've been confronted by angry male contributors, all of whom seem to be over 6 feet tall, who've demanded to know why the hell I didn't use their ideas (this never seems to happen to Nancy). But our selections are based on usefulness, imagination, and clarity of presentation. After 17 years of cruising, if neither of us can understand it, there's probably something missing.

I found myself on the wrong end of the horse with a TTW contribution I made before becoming the editor of the section. A friend had solved the black-mark problem caused by the rub strake on his inflatable. After topside abuse had cost him several close friends, he painted his rub strake with a thick, white, water-based paint used to paint chain and anchors. I saw that it worked on his dinghy, and he assured me it had lasted for a couple of years. There was a special preparation involved which I followed to the letter. Happy with the result, three months later I sent in the idea. Ah—too soon, which is why we have the "it has to have worked for a year" condition. After six months the paint on my dinghy's rub strake began to peel off. Much to my chagrin, this solution that didn't work as well as I'd claimed was included in the first book, *SAIL's Things That Work,* and remains a permanent source of embarrassment.

One last tale: A contributor sent in an idea for keeping mud wasps from building a nest in his outboard air intake. It was amusingly presented, but we rejected the idea, figuring that, of SAIL's hundreds of thousands of readers, maybe one reader at most would find mud-wasp defense relevant. Six months later we discovered we couldn't fill one of our water tanks. Why? Because a X@#! mud wasp had plugged the vent!

Nevertheless, in spite of karma, personal fallibility, and other human considerations, we've put together this compendium of ideas that their donors claim to have worked. Because many ideas are boat-specific, only some will work for you. At least a few, we hope, will zap a synapse.

To our contributors, then, we thank you; to tinkerer-putterers, don't be shy—we welcome your contributions; and to sailors everywhere, we herewith offer a read designed to roust the mind and engage the imagination.

—Herb and Nancy Payson

CONTENTS

Maintenance

Systems

Water treatment	2
Potable water	2
Bleach on demand	2
Water-tank maintenance	3
Hands-free head cleaning	3
Holding-tank pumpout aid	4
Clearing the holding tank	4
Eliminate head odors	5
Solving a holding-tank dilemma	5
Pumpout problem	6
Winning the fight against head odors	6
Head deodorizer	6
"Roto-Rooter" replaced	7
"Drano" for intakes	7
Impromptu gaskets	8
Bolts in cramped areas	8
Dimples that can save your blocks	8
Difficult nuts and bolts	9
Dealing with pipe and hose	10
Declawing wire ties	11
Wire-nut connectors	11
Wire-nut trick	12
Soldering tip	12
Protection for electrical connections	12
Gelcoat repair	13
Glass cleaning	14

Cleaning tips	14
Cleaner	14
Clean the sticky	14
Replacing steering cables	15
Fixing a leaky rudderpost	16
Testing for rigging flaws	17
Spit-and-polish brass	18
Add battery water without spills	18

Powertrain/Fuel

Impeller installation	19
Avoiding diesel spills	19
Help for a fuel-filter change	19
Color-coded tools	20
Containing an oil change	20
Neat oil change	21
An easy oil funnel	22
Diaper dandy	22
Oil-filter removal	22
Oil change made easy	23
Oil-change tip	24
Fuel-line washer renewal	24
Eyebolts instead of padeyes	24
Freshwater flush	25
Cutless bearing	26
Prop-shaft packing removal	27
Repacking the shaft gland	27
Fluid filler	27

Winter Storage

Take cover   28
Improved tie-downs   29
Adjustable tie-downs   29
Long-lasting tie-downs   29
Tie-down quickie   30
Furler protection   30
No more frozen water lines   31
Fluid control   32

Modifications and Installations

Electronics/Electrical

Hinged instrument panel   34
Water-resistant GPS   35
Handy GPS and speaker mount   35
Compass corruption   36
Cockpit VHF audio   36
Taming the through-hull geyser   36
Avoid through-hull drilling   37
Solar-panel mount   38
Simple wire-leading   39
Spare-pump wiring   39
Protect your pump   39
Autopilot case   40
Mobile radar mount   41
VHF holder   41
Breaker breaker   42
Diskette rehab   42
More cockpit space for tiller boats   43

Ground Tackle/Docking

Homemade flopper stopper   44
Milk-crate stairs   45
Chafing protection   45
More anchor light   45
Controlling your anchor buoy   46
Dockline saver   47
Bowsprit protection   48
Chafing gear   48
A bridle for chain rode   49
Anchor-chain stopper   50
Fender rig   50
Building a fender board   51
Removable anchor-rode locker   52
Efficient ground-tackle storage   53
Lunch-hook storage   54
Bird barrier   54
Bird ban(ners)   54
Aesthetic bird barrier   55
Bird whacker   56
Happier birds, clean deck   57

Exterior

Scrub-a-dub-dub   58
Protect your fingers   59
Hand-sanding tool   59

Bottom sanding within reach 59
Do-it-yourself custom lettering 60
Removing tape 60
Through-the-deck fittings 61
Hatch screen I 61
Hatch screen II 62
Tiller stiller 63
Tiller extension 64
Tiller-extension tamer 65
Lifeline cosmetics 65
Stronger stanchions 66
Custom stanchion fittings 66
Securing lifelines 67
Comfort on the rail 68
Cockpit table I 69
Cockpit table for boats with tillers 70
Cockpit/saloon table 71
Cockpit table II 72
Custom-fitted cockpit drink holder 73
More light in the cabin 74
Polishing Lexan 74
Binnacle cover 75
Cockpit-instrument covers 75
Instrument-panel protection 76
Portlight covers 77
Lazaret-lid holder 78
Removable cockpit-cushion covers 78
Custom helm seat 79
Under-the-seat stowage 80
Winch-handle holders 81
Stovepipe hat 81
Vent restrainers 81
Shock-absorbing padeye 82

Boom support 83
Boom crutch 84
Inexpensive hand-rail covers 84
Instant cockpit cover and more 85
Dodger guard 86

Painting/Adhesives

Bottom painting 87
Propeller fouling 87
Seized seizing 87
Mixing small quantities of epoxy 88
Varnish-removal aid 88
Drip-proof varnish pot 89
Varnish touch-up 89
Freezer brush and paint storage 89

Rigging

Line hangers 90
Rings instead of pins 90
Line cutter/soldering gun 90
Rope-work tool 91
Clean-cut lines 91
Whipping with floss 91
A modern monkey fist 92
Easier masthead work 93
A more comfortable bosun's chair 94
Gybe, no! 94
Topping-lift control 95
No more flopping topping lifts 96
Topping-lift ring 97
Storing a removable staysail stay 98
Make your own spreader boots 99
Do-it-yourself shroud covers 100

No more cleat hangups   100
Reefing aid for roller-reefing jibs   101
Halyard wrap on a roller-furler?   102
No more halyard wrap   102
Inexpensive shroud cleats   103
Midship cleat   103
Cutting rigging wire   104
Cutting wire rope   104

Sails

Tie-downs for mainsails   105
Roller-furling headsail security   106
Genoa-track alternative   106
Jib net   107
Ripstop nylon-drifter repair   108
Canvas closure   108
No more rusty sewing needles   108
Easier reefing   109
Reefing convenience   110
S'nuff said   111
Easy spinnaker handling   112
Small-boat whisker pole   113
Batten storage   114
No more battens overboard   114
Rigid sail bags   115
Sail folding made simple   116

Interior

Centerboard pusher   117
Socket organizer   118
Small-parts storage   118
Locker locks   118
Hatchboard stowage   118

Hatchboard holder   119
Removable anti-skid   120
Uncrazing hatches and ports   120
Keeping cushions in place   121
More privacy   121
Convenient carry-all   121
Water heater plus   122
City water pressure   123
Flying-object holder   123
Icebox drain   124
Combination pump   125
Add counter space   125

Trailersailing

Anti-skid for an outboard fuel tank   126
Stop gas tanks from sliding   126
Outboard starter   126
Outboard tilting made easier   127
Quick shifter   128
Cure that broken step   129
Cockpit-sole grate as berth   129
Trailering security for rigging   130
Mast silencer   130
Silencing nocturnal mast knock   130
Trailer-tongue extension   131
Foolproof launching   132
Pressurized spray   132
Easy electrical power   132
Pole storage   133
Mast-stepping aid   133

Techniques for Cruisers

Anchoring, Docking, Mooring

Piling pointers	135
Fail-safe docking	136
Position marks on lines	137
Using enough snubber	137
Singlehanded mooring pickup	138
Docking technique	138
Singlehanded docking	139
Backing in safely	140
Simplified mooring pickup	141
Singlehanded anchoring	141
Cut-the-shouting headset	142
Remote tiller steering	143

Creating storage

Space saver	144
Cowboy-style storage	144
Settee storage	144
Coffee table with storage	145
Small-boat hangups	145
Book holder	146
Handy storage	147
More storage	148
Boathook storage	148

Galley Innovations

No more spilled drinks	149
A sink-mounted drink holder	149
Wine-glass storage	150
Utensil and plate box	151
The not-so-trivial trivet	152
Ice-cold water on demand	153
Ice for coffee?	154
No-effort potato rinsing	155
Hibachi help	155
Jar protection	155
No more skidding dishes	155
Instant ice	156
Extending veggie life	156
Flatware storage	157
Dispensing with trays	157
Taming the gimballed stove	158
Cooking-alcohol container	159
Easy fill for alcohol stoves	160
Fuel-gauge alternative	160
Propane abroad	161

Life at Anchor (Tips for Cruisers)

Catching rain	162
Bimini help	162
Awning-water collection	162
Quieting transom slap	163

Goof retrieval   163
Boater's bubble bath   163
Hat preservation   164
Hat-on-the-head trick   164
The rat race   164
Anti-cockroach tactic   164
Clean cats afloat   165
An inspired flag halyard   166
Flag care   167
Photo postcards   167
Quick-dry towels   167
Fishanasia   167

Navigation/Charts

Chart magnifier   168
Portable chart table I   168
Portable chart table II   169
Portable chart table III   170
Keep rolled-up charts flat   170
Chart in the cockpit   170
Do-it-yourself waterproof charts   171
Chart loans   171
Full-color chart markers   171
Post-it Notes for chart work   171

Safety Issues/ Organization

Man-overboard float   172
Emergency steering   172
Singlehander's last-chance lanyard   173
Impromptu engine cooling   174
Low-cost security   174
Rudder-loss protection   174

PFD cushions   175
Cockpit-locker lock   175
It's a lock   176
Organization map   176
Universal status board   177
Log plus   177
Organization solution   178
Organizing boat papers   178

Dinghy Works

Dinghy boarding ladder   179
Outboard dolly   180
Eliminate black marks   180
Outboard hoist   181
Primary care for inflatables   182
Just for kicks   182
Dollar dinghy drain   183
Dinghy control   184
Tame that towed dinghy   184
Towing rudder for inflatable dinghies   185
Dinghy oar rack   186
Dinghy fenders   187

Index   188

Maintenance

This section begins with two ideas you can contemplate over a plate of eggs and bacon. We recommend, however, reading about heads and holding tanks after you've left the table—unless you tend not to visualize the way I do. Incidentally, I do have an idea about heads that never made SAIL Magazine's Things That Work: When we were cruising on *Sea Foam,* our 36-foot Angleman/Davies wooden ketch, we invented a method of pumping a broken head dry. One day the flapper refused to close, so the pump stroke (that pushed the piston up) created a geyser of sewage. What was needed was a way to block the hole during one half of the stroke and to unblock it for the other half. Our solution was a tennis ball on a stick, or in desperate times, an orange and rubber gloves. There were several indescribable disasters during our learning period, but you can be sure that the orange was subsequently discarded. I've always felt I missed an opportunity by not submitting this idea.

A messy if less noxious job is dealing with engine fluids, and we've included several excellent suggestions that can help you do engine chores more efficiently. There's plenty of information about how to install new packing in the stuffing box—we've included

an excellent method for making the flax circlets exactly the right size, a method that I found both easier and less frustrating than using pi, diameters, and a calculator. But I'd never heard any advice on how you get the flax out until a reader came up with the idea that you'll read in the pages to follow.

I'll bet you'd be upset if you came alongside my boat and asked to borrow some grommets for your winter boat cover and I gave you a tennis ball—you would be, that is, until you read the idea submitted by Raymond Weber. He claims the boy scouts have always known about this use for tennis balls, but my troop leader didn't, or if he did he never passed the idea along to me.

Maintenance can be a pain or a pleasure. I personally have never felt the rewards of "a good job well done" until it was done. During maintenance chores I usually experience only anxiety, disappointment, and frustration. However, I've found that new ideas are fun and help to make the process as rewarding as its completion. I hope the suggestions here help you to a new and less foreboding approach to the necessary task of keeping your boat in shippy shape; perhaps they'll inspire you to invent solutions of your own.

Systems

Water treatment

Reader Jack Morton, who sails *Fanny II,* an Irwin 10/4 out of Nassau Bay, Texas, was never quite sure if he'd used enough bleach to kill all the beasties in his water tank. He generally uses six drops of 6-percent bleach solution per gallon of water but writes, "I'm not too faithful with the administration of these drops. After all, my water source is pure and contamination isn't usually a problem in a small, closed system [like mine]. To be sure that the tank has suitable chlorine levels [to prevent bacteria growth], I use the same test kit that I use on our swimming pool."

Jack mixes a sample of *Fanny II*'s tank water with a pool chemical that alters the color of the sample based on its chlorine concentration. He then compares his sample to a reference scale (included with the pool kit) to determine the chlorine concentration. He warns that the sample should not then be re-introduced into the water tank, because the pool chemical is toxic. "After adding the drops of bleach I think I need to a ½ gallon of water, I pour it into the tank. If I've inadvertently used too much chlorine, I use a charcoal filter to filter the water for drinking until I can add more fresh water."

Potable water

No matter how carefully you fill your water tanks and add chlorine to prevent algae, solids will eventually build up in the tank. This won't be noticeable until the tank is nearly empty and you're in rough seas, at which time the water may come out full of sediment. When this happens, we've had to use coffee filters to get a clear glass of water.

Floridian Edward Manzer had a better idea for *Rum Line,* his Gulfstar 37. He installed two filters—one a cotton-type filter, the other a carbon type—in series. The first eliminates particles; the second takes out bad odors and taste. He adds, "It also keeps a lot of junk out of your pumps."

Bleach on demand

Scott White of Fort Lauderdale, Florida, adds storage space by shrinking that which needs to be stored—in this case, chlorine bleach. He buys swimming-pool chlorinating tablets ($.50 each) at his local pool-supply store and then breaks off a couple of sugar cube–size chunks, drops them into a (small) bleach bottle, adds water, and shakes it up. Presto—instant bleach in controlled concentrations. White says that two tablets have lasted over a year. Another advantage, he claims, is that while bottled bleach loses strength over time, the tablets retain full strength until water is added.

Water-tank maintenance

Chlorine is out, Dr. Jerry Kaifetz tells us, and hydrogen peroxide is in. Jerry, who sails *Sunshine,* an Irwin 32, out of East Chicago, says, "Because bleach is toxic to humans, hydrogen peroxide is better as a disinfectant." To maintain freshness in his boat's water tank, he uses between ½ and 1 ounce of a 27 percent hydrogen-peroxide solution (available at most pool-supply stores) per 10 gallons of water. Higher concentrations can be used for corrective rather than for maintenance purposes. Dr. Kaifetz claims that if you use too much hydrogen peroxide, there will be a harmless but chemical taste to the water, which can be eliminated by draining some of the water from the tank and replacing it with fresh water. He notes that hydrogen peroxide is relatively inexpensive compared with bleach, considering how little is required to do the job.

Hands-free head cleaning

Laura Ellis sails *Sudden Impulse,* a 65-footer based in Cape Canaveral, Florida. She noticed that polluted water left an ugly stain in the bowl of her boat's MSD. Not one to scrub, Laura simply tosses a couple of denture-cleaning tablets into the bowl to bubble away the stain. A word of caution: Don't flush until the pill has completely dissolved; wait several hours.

Holding-tank pumpout aid

Larry Watkins has observed that sometimes the sewage in his holding tank refuses to be pumped overboard or removed at a pumpout station. Without going too deeply into detail, this is no doubt a question of viscosity. Larry's solution is to help the pumpout process by compressing the air in the holding tank. He uses a foot pump attached either to the vent or, with the vent hose removed, directly to the vent fitting on the holding tank. He then turns on the overboard or pumpout pump and steps on the foot pump several times, creating enough pressure to push the sewage into the holding tank's outlet. Once the sewage is flowing, he keeps up a steady pressure with his foot until the holding tank is empty. Larry cautions that compressed air is powerful and that some holding tanks are made only of thin plastic.

Clearing the holding tank

A clothes pin (for your nose) is about the only tool most of us want for pumping out a holding tank. Unfortunately, solids can settle and block the exit pipe, meaning that it's time for some dirty business. George Reed, who skippers a Nonsuch 30 out of Edenton, North Carolina, put together a device to clear up blockages using a garden hose and a length of soft copper tubing. He purchased a shut-off valve at the local hardware store and screwed it onto the end of his dockside garden hose. He then mated 18 inches of copper tubing to the valve, using fittings that were also purchased at the hardware store. To clear a blockage, he inserts the tubing into the tank through the intake and directs the water jet at the blockage. The shut-off valve can be used to regulate the water pressure, and the tubing can be shaped to reach any corner of the tank. A few seconds of the water jet will usually dissolve most blockages so the tank can be pumped out.

Eliminate head odors

Salt water can cause foul head odors in a stored boat, no matter how well you clean the head. This is usually the result of organisms living and dying in the plumbing, as well as accumulated slime in the head itself. Aboard his Hunter 375, *NY Cool,* Arthur Wener solved the problem with a combination of fresh water and head deodorant. When he leaves his boat for extended periods, Wener disconnects the seawater-intake hose and pumps several bowls full of fresh water and deodorant through the entire system. During the winter layup he does this before adding antifreeze. Wener says, "Salt water in the bowl will give off foul odors after a few days. Fresh water with deodorant will smell fresh for weeks, and the hoses between the bowl and the holding tank won't give off unwanted odors."

A *Red Shoes* hint: Rather than disconnect the seawater intake, a garden hose connected to dock water and pushed into the intake from the outside will deodorize the intake hose as well.

Solving a holding-tank dilemma

George Peterson has a 50-gallon holding tank on his Pearson 365 ketch, *Matiness II,* which he sails on the Great Lakes. He used to wonder if a second rinse after a pumpout was necessary to fully clean the tank. After constructing a removable see-through connector for the deck fitting, however, he wonders no more. George made the connector with a 6-inch length of $1\frac{7}{8}$-inch clear vinyl tubing (to meet USCG regulations, the tubing must be at least as strong as the pipe that leads from the holding tank to the deck fitting), one $1\frac{1}{2}$-inch PVC-1 hose-to-pipe adapter, and one $1\frac{1}{2}$-inch pipe-thread PVC-1 pipe-to-hose adapter. He fitted the clear hose between the two adapters.

To pump out, he screws the "male" adapter into the deck plate and the pumpout hose into the "female" adapter. During the pumpout the effluent is visible through the clear hose, and it's easy to see if the tank needs a second rinse. Before you undertake this project, George advises, take the cap from your deck fitting to a hardware store to make sure that your boat's deck fittings are standard pipe thread. An improper fit could be catastrophic and, well, messy.

Pumpout problem

Charles Cable of Strongsville, Ohio, solved a potentially messy problem when the pumpout fitting on the deck of his boat, *Time,* failed to seal. He used a dock hose to direct a stream of water at the fitting, which sealed the air out and allowed the pump to generate enough suction to get the job done until the fitting could be fixed.

Winning the fight against head odors

When a boat is closed up, the head and related plumbing will often fill the boat's interior with bad smells. The solution: Put mothballs into plastic margarine containers, the tops of which have been vented with large holes, says Chuck Delabio, who sails *Chinook,* a CS-33. He places these containers in the head compartment, vanity cupboard, and next to the holding tank. Chuck claims his method is cheaper, more effective, and produces a more pleasant odor than commercial deodorizers.

Head deodorizer

Ted Arnold, of Sarasota, Florida, has a good idea for counteracting odors in the head aboard *Phantom,* his O'Day 25. Because he dislikes the perfumed smell of commercial deodorizers, he bought a bottle of vanilla extract from the local supermarket. He added a wick made of several pieces of cotton twine to the bottle, using enough pieces to fill the neck of the bottle without crowding. "Leave a quarter-inch of the wick sticking out," Ted says, "and enjoy the aroma."

"Roto-Rooter" replaced

Art Wener of Jericho, New York, has an interesting method for clearing stopped hoses, lines, drains, clogged through-hull piping, and the like, that can't be snaked out due to 90-degree turns. He has discovered that a manual (or electric) air pump for inflating dinghies comes with tapered plastic fittings of various sizes. By inserting one of these fittings into the hose and pumping air into the line, most stoppages can be cleared out. It's also possible with some pumps to do the reverse and suck the stoppage through.

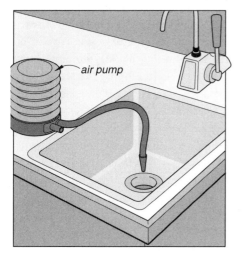

"Drano" for intakes

A quickie comes from Paul Ayer of San Clemente, California, who was troubled by an overheating engine aboard his Schock 34 on the return trip from the Newport–Ensenada Race. He discovered that kelp on the raw-water intake strainer was the culprit. To fix the problem without getting wet, he removed one end of the raw-water hose from the impeller housing and stuck the end of the hose into his air horn. Two quick blasts cleared the clog. You can also use an inflatable-dinghy pump in the same way. We've used our ruggedly built Avon pump several times to unclog *Red Shoes*'s intake strainers.

Impromptu gaskets

William Rossberger of Chicago, Illinois, sails a Scampi 30 and offers this suggestion for an emergency gasket. William couldn't locate a gasket for his bulkhead-mounted compass, so he made one out of a plastic-container lid, cutting accurate circles by using a circle, or "fly," cutter with an electric drill.

Bolts in cramped areas

While replacing a genoa track in a hard-to-reach area aboard *Time,* Charles Cable found that there was too little space between headliner and deck to use anything except a box wrench. It was impossible to get his hand in to thread the nut, and socket wrenches were too big. Charles was finally able to thread the nut and hold it by putting a piece of masking tape over the bottom of the box wrench. This held the nut while he placed it over the end of the bolt and a partner turned the bolt from topside.

Dimples that can save your blocks

Charles Rice of Goldsboro, North Carolina, remembered the skinned knees he got as a youngster when the nuts vibrated loose from his roller skates and the wheels fell off. He solved that problem by putting the point of a steel punch into the thread seam between the nut and the axle and giving it a sharp blow with a hammer, which left a dimple in the metal that locked the nut in place. Now that he sails and no longer skates, the same dimples have found their way onto his boat.

To keep deck hardware from being stolen when he leaves his boat unattended, Charles puts three large dimples, 120 degrees apart, at the threaded end of the shackles holding the jibsheet-lead blocks. Removing the screw from the shackle now requires two large wrenches. The same dimples will act as locks to keep any nut, such as engine-mounting nuts and the nuts bolting your spreaders to the mast, from backing off because of vibration; adding security will cost nothing but a sharp tap with a hammer and a steel punch.

Difficult nuts and bolts

This is one of the most helpful and simple ideas I've seen in awhile, and I can only wonder where the author, Francis Cichowski, was when we began cruising. Cichowski, who sails *Southern Comfort,* a Cal 34-3, writes from Connecticut, "I was at the dock, attempting to reinstall my primary cooling pump. Its location is so inconvenient that I could either bend to see the bolt holes or reach to touch them—but not both. To make things worse, the bolt installs head down, and the fully inserted bolt leaves insufficient room to install the nut."

His solution was to snake dental floss through the bolt hole and tie the snaked end of the floss to the threaded end of the bolt (see illustration). This allowed Cichowski to pull the bolt into position with the floss and to maintain tension. He threaded the washer and nut onto the floss and slid them down to the bolt. He then spun the nut onto the bolt, let it shear the floss from the bolt, and tightened the assembly as required.

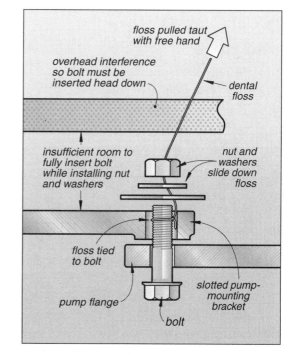

floss pulled taut with free hand

overhead interference so bolt must be inserted head down

dental floss

insufficient room to fully insert bolt while installing nut and washers

nut and washers slide down floss

floss tied to bolt

pump flange

slotted pump-mounting bracket

bolt

Dealing with pipe and hose

Some helpful suggestions for cutting PVC pipe come from Conrad Skladal, who with his wife, Charlotte, recently completed a 15-year circumnavigation on *Wisp,* a 43-foot

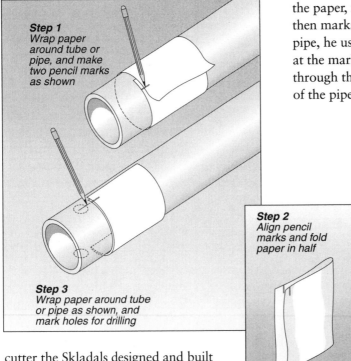

Step 1
Wrap paper around tube or pipe, and make two pencil marks as shown

Step 3
Wrap paper around tube or pipe as shown, and mark holes for drilling

Step 2
Align pencil marks and fold paper in half

cutter the Skladals designed and built themselves. To make a square cut on any tubular or round item, he uses a hose clamp as a guide. If the pipe is too large or if a hose clamp isn't available, he wraps a

piece of typing paper around the object and traces around the edge with a marker.

Most interesting to me was Conrad's technique for drilling a hole through the tube's axis. He wraps the tube with a sheet of paper as before and makes two pencil marks, which designate the pipe's circumference (see illustration), on the edge of the paper. He removes the paper, folds it so the marks align, and then marks the crease. After rewrapping the pipe, he uses a center punch to score the pipe at the marks on the paper. The holes drilled through these marks will go through the axis of the pipe.

Declawing wire ties

Roy Hanson, who sails *Cream Puff,* an Island Packet 35, out of North Carolina, got tired of getting scratched by the snipped-off ends of plastic wire ties. After a day of wire-tie encounters, his wife told him he looked like he'd lost a cat fight. His solution? When cutting the excess from the ends, leave about $3/8$ inch extra. Then trim with a pair of nail clippers. The edge will be smooth, and the curve will keep the offending corners out of the way.

Wire-nut connectors

An idea that we use on *Red Shoes* comes from Steve Blunden, who's used it for the last decade on his C&C 29, *Twilight Zone.* Although soldering is a secure way to join two wires, it's also permanent and often difficult to do onboard unless you have access to shore power. Blunden's solution is to use wire nuts (plastic cones containing a small spring that screws down over the wire ends) to make a secure mechanical/electrical connection. The problem with wire nuts is that, because they are generally used in house (not marine) construction, the spring inside corrodes easily. Blunden, who hails from Madison, Connecticut, solves this problem by filling the wire nut with silicon sealant after assembling the connection. This gives him a water-resistant connection that can be taken apart and reassembled with minimum difficulty.

Wire-nut trick

Having tried to cram sealant into wire nuts after they're attached (and in the process spread goo all over my hands and the surrounding area), I'm particularly grateful for Edward Manzer's simple solution. Ed sails *Rum Line,* his Gulfstar 37, out of Royal Palm Beach, Florida, and fills the wire nuts with sealant before putting them on. A caveat: If you have to disconnect the nuts because you forgot to add a wire, you may still have to deal with a mess.

Although wire nuts are designed to be used with house, or solid-strand, wire (not with multi-strand marine wire), we've used wire nuts on *Red Shoes* for years. In disassembling connections from time to time I've never—that's never—seen any evidence of damage to the strands.

Soldering tip

If the tip of your soldering iron has accumulated too many impurities to heat properly, here's a idea from Arthur Lee of Santa Cruz, California, that we use on *Red Shoes*. Art heats his iron, lets it cool a bit, and wipes the tip with a damp sponge, or "scrubby," leaving the tip bright and shiny for the next job.

Protection for electrical connections

Charles C. Squires of Kilmaranock, Virginia, tells us that he hears a lot of complaints about electronic equipment on boats. "Failure is usually caused by corroded connections. I think I've solved a big part of these troubles on my boat.

"Start by cleaning the connection until it's shiny. Make a good, tight joint, and then paint the area with fingernail polish. Voila! You have a color-coded, watertight seal that will last a long time."

Gelcoat repair

Sometimes an idea that's pure gold comes along. Ted Kurtz of Northampton, Massachusetts, who maintains his Crealock 34 with meticulous care, discovered that finishing a ding repair with fine wet-and-dry sandpaper was time-consuming and always removed some of the surrounding (undamaged) gelcoat. Ted suggests the following process as an alternative.

Clean the area to be repaired with soapy water, rinse, and let dry. Apply catalyzed gelcoat to the dings with a suitable tool—Ted uses a screwdriver—leaving a small lump of gelcoat. After the gelcoat sets, wax the repaired area (the wax acts as a lubricant for the blade). Put masking tape over the sharp ends of a utility-knife blade as shown to protect your hands. Lift the blade (slightly) off the surface of the gelcoat, and use the blade to level the repair, making several passes to gradually shave the lump. Apply a combination rubbing compound/wax product, which renders the repair invisible. Ted maintains that the shaving process takes only seconds and leaves the healthy gelcoat unaffected.

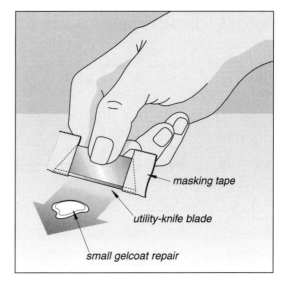

masking tape

utility-knife blade

small gelcoat repair

Glass cleaning

An idea that I learned as a young man but that may have escaped the younger generation comes from Gwen Bylund, who lives in Mamaris, Turkey, aboard *Hellem Nooh*. When cleaning and drying mirrors or portlights with vinegar, Windex, or the like, use a lightly crushed ball of newspaper. Cloth or paper towels leave lint on the glass; newsprint does not.

Cleaning tips

Bette Huber of Knoxville, Tennessee, sails *Sirene,* a Catalina 30, and has found many uses for the fishnet-like nylon netting she buys at fabric stores. She tells us that whitewall tire cleaner, with nylon netting as a scrubber, will clean the foulest of fenders. She also uses nylon netting and a touch of acetone to remove masking-tape glue from fiberglass. Bette claims that using a bar of Ivory soap wrapped in nylon netting makes cleaning the boat above and below the waterline a breeze.

Cleaner

A quickie from Curtis Basye, who sails *Quintessence,* a Hunter 26, out of Buck Creek, Ohio. He reminds us that a mechanic's hand cleaner (such as Gunk) will clean oil and tar off a fiberglass hull.

Clean the sticky

John and Wendy Harpool, who sail *Lazy Days,* a Hunter 22, out of Winslow, Maine, claim that Avon's Skin So Soft is good at removing the sticky residue from electrical tape.

Replacing steering cables

I'm going to remember this one if, God forbid, I ever have to replace the cables in my Edson steering pedestal. Chuck Cable, who sails *Time,* an Express 35, out of Strongsville, Ohio, suggests an easy way to run new steering cables. Use split-PVC tubing (like the cable covers found in the West Marine or Davis Instruments catalogues) with a slightly larger inner diameter than the cable to be replaced. The PVC is rigid enough to be pushed up from the backing plate at the bottom of the pedestal to the top of the pedestal. With the PVC in place, it's a simple matter to push the limp cables down from the top of the pedestal through the tubes. Finally, pull out the tubing, which is already split, leaving the new cables in place.

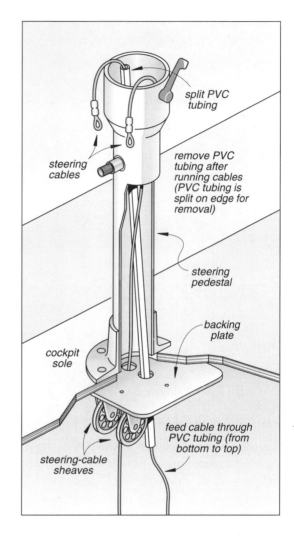

split PVC tubing

steering cables

remove PVC tubing after running cables (PVC tubing is split on edge for removal)

steering pedestal

backing plate

cockpit sole

feed cable through PVC tubing (from bottom to top)

steering-cable sheaves

Fixing a leaky rudderpost

Charles H. Cook, Jr. of New Wilington, Pennsylvania, has found a do-it-yourself solution for an inboard rudderpost leak aboard

The split can be sealed with fiberglass tape, epoxy resin, and/or epoxy putty after the sleeve is fitted into place. The ends of this sleeve are sealed to the bottom of the cockpit sole and the inside bottom of the hull with the same materials. WEST System compounds work well. A few wraps of tape will hold the split closed while the seal sets. Once installed, this sleeve harmlessly confines any water that squeezes through the rudderpost bearing.

tiller

cockpit

rudderpost

4" ABS tubing

hull

rudder

seal ABS tubing to hull and bottom of cockpit sole with thickened epoxy

his tiller-steered boat. For a waterproof sleeve he used a piece of semi-flexible ABS plastic tubing with an inside diameter just larger than the outside diameter of the rudderpost. He cut the sleeve to a length that reaches from the inside of the hull to the underside of the cockpit sole. Then he split the sleeve lengthwise to allow it to be fitted over the rudderpost.

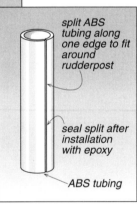

split ABS tubing along one edge to fit around rudderpost

seal split after installation with epoxy

ABS tubing

Testing for rigging flaws

Gregory Anstey of Wilmot, Nova Scotia, has devised an inexpensive test for locating rigging-terminal flaws.

Start with a can of everyday penetrating oil, and mix in just enough black or red dye powder to color the oil. Apply the mixture to the end fittings with a soft brush and let stand for approximately 20 minutes. Use a rag dampened (not soaked) with a solvent, such as alcohol, to remove the excess oil/dye mixture from the fitting. Then apply a light coat of talcum or baby powder to the fitting and let it stand approximately 10 minutes. Now you're ready to inspect the fittings; a crack will appear as a red or black (depending on the dye used) line on the powder.

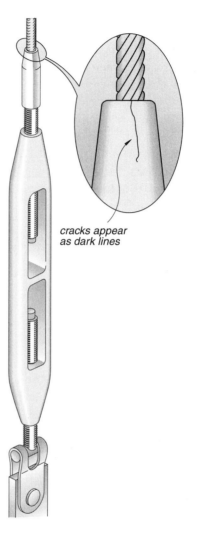

cracks appear as dark lines

Spit-and-polish brass

Anything that makes polishing bronze or brass easier is welcome information. Gwen Bylund, who lives aboard *Helem Nooh* in Marmaris, Turkey, says she gets good results using fine-grade, wet-and-dry sandpaper and spit (or a drop of water). It's quicker than other methods, and she claims it works better than commercial polishes. We suggest trying this with different grades of sandpaper on a piece of scrap bronze until you find a grade that doesn't scratch but that is still abrasive enough to get the job done.

Add battery water without spills

If you carry distilled water to top off your lead-acid batteries, you might find the water difficult to dispense. James Strom fills his batteries with a plastic squeeze bottle normally used by cyclists to carry drinking water. If the batteries are in an awkward position, making filling difficult even with the squeeze bottle, attach a piece of narrow-diameter hose to the nipple on the cap of the squeeze bottle. The bracket that normally attaches this type of bottle to a bicycle frame can be mounted to any bulkhead to keep the bottle within easy reach. Strom, who sails *Paper Clipper,* his Irwin 38, near Jamison, Pennsylvania, uses another squeeze bottle to top off his cooling-water reservoir but advises that, in order to avoid contamination, any distilled-water bottle not be used for other purposes.

Powertrain/Fuel

Impeller installation

An apparently well-known but new-to-us method for installing a pump impeller comes from Richard Megregian of Farmington Hills, Michigan. The challenge is to get all the impeller vanes bent in the right direction. To accomplish this, Richard uses a hose clamp the same circumference as the impeller and controls which way the vanes bend with a finger as he tightens the clamp. Since he lubes the vanes with a water-based lubricant, it's a simple matter to slide the impeller out of the clamp and into the pump housing. Megregian sails *Hye-n-Mighty,* a Catalina 28, and always keeps a spare impeller and hose clamp on board.

Avoiding diesel spills

An innovative idea for avoiding diesel spills when refueling with a jerry jug comes from Doug Niedt of St. Louis, Missouri. Doug makes a shallow dish from aluminum foil that fits in the space around the filler pipe. He then places the foil over the filler hole, cuts an "X" through the foil over the opening, and inserts the funnel through the "X." If the fuel spills, it will collect in the foil dish, which can be rolled up and disposed of in an ecologically correct manner.

Help for a fuel-filter change

Stephen Dilendick from Stoneham, Massachusetts, came up with an idea I've seen (in differing versions) on several sailboats. The owner of a Hunter 30, *Triple Take,* Stephen hated the inconvenience of pouring diesel into the cleaned filter housing and then bleeding the air from the lines. He alleviated the problem by adding an outboard primer bulb upstream of the first fuel filter. After removing the dirty element and cleaning the filter bowl, he inserts a new filter and fills the bowl by squeezing the primer bulb. With the filter top screwed on, he then bleeds the air that changing the fuel filter has introduced to the fuel lines.

On *Red Shoes* we have an electric fuel pump that allows us to bleed the lines using the magic of amperes. Filling the filter bowl, however, has always been an awkward chore, and, thanks to Stephen, my shopping list now includes a spare outboard primer bulb.

Color-coded tools

For people who don't use their boats as often as they'd like, this idea from Robert Anstiss might make some sense. Anstiss found that bleeding the air from his diesel engine's fuel system required several wrenches. He also found that too much sediment in the bottom of his fuel tank tended to block the fuel intake just when he needed engine power to keep a heavy current from pushing the boat into disaster. To get to the correct tools in a hurry, he color-coded the nuts and wrenches with bright paint. Now he reaches for the green wrench to tighten the green nut, and so on. Robert has cruised his 30-foot wooden staysail ketch, *"D" Vara,* from Mobile Bay to Lake Michigan.

Containing an oil change

From Brian Keenan of St. Paul, Minnesota, skipper of *Aoelia,* a Johnson J Scow, comes this oil-change suggestion. Before changing the oil filter, pump the oil out of the crankcase. Place a small container (one that won't melt when filled with hot engine oil) under the oil filter, and punch a hole in the lowest point of the filter with an awl or screwdriver. To reduce spillage when the filter is unscrewed from the engine, let the oil drain into the container before the filter is removed.

Neat oil change

From Ed Reed of Kennewick, Washington, comes a neat solution to messy oil changes (see illustration). All he needed was a gallon paint can, two tire-valve stems, and a manual oil-change pump. "First I removed the valves from the stems. To improve the seal for the pump, I filed the threads off the outside of the stems by jamming a bolt into the stem, chucking the bolt head into my electric drill, and using a file to remove the threads while the drill spun the stem." Reed drilled two holes (the same diameter as the stems) into the paint-can lid, inserted the stems, and sealed them with epoxy. He inserted a straight (and clean) piece of copper tubing—which won't curl in hot oil—into the crankcase through the dipstick hole. A piece of vinyl tubing connects the copper tubing to one of the stems on the paint can. He attached the pump to the other stem with another length of vinyl tubing. As he manipulates the pump, the oil is sucked into the can. "The pump stays clean, it's noiseless until the final slurp, and it doesn't need electricity," says Reed, who sails *Fat Cat*, a San Juan 34. He uses the can to store the oil until he can dispose of it properly.

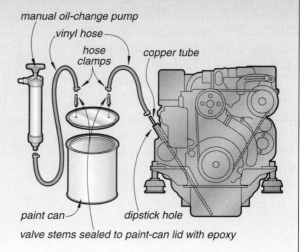

manual oil-change pump

vinyl hose

hose clamps

copper tube

paint can

dipstick hole

valve stems sealed to paint-can lid with epoxy

An easy oil funnel

On *Red Shoes,* as on many sailboats we've seen, the engine's oil-funnel hole is close enough to a structural member to make use of a normal funnel impossible. Quentin Kinderman, who sails *Clairebuoyant,* a Pearson 36, out of Edgewater, Maryland, recommends making a broad, shallow funnel by cutting the top 3 inches off a plastic Evian water bottle. Kinderman claims that the mouth of the bottle fits nicely into the oil-filler hole and makes adding oil easy.

Diaper dandy

From Carolyn Corbett comes this super idea. When changing the oil on her marine diesel, she puts a disposable diaper in the engine pan. She uses another diaper to grasp the filter and wipe oil dribbles off the engine. Carolyn sails *Bifrost,* a Morgan 41, out of Backus, Minnesota.

Oil-filter removal

The dock master of George Randig's marina told him to use the leather belt that was holding up his (George's) pants, because he didn't have a tool for removing a hard-to-get-off oil filter aboard his Catalina 36. The belt was easy to place around the filter and worked even better than the wrench that's designed for the job. The only problem, says George, is that in the excitement of triumph over your oil filter, your (beltless) pants may fall down. From a *Red Shoes* perspective, we feel that embarrassment is a small price to pay for success, and that the accidental mooning of unhelpful crewmembers who consider oily messes funny is indeed appropriate.

Oil change made easy

While changing his engine's oil using a hand pump, Jim Lauser of Media, Pennsylvania, found that he needed "one hand to hold the neoprene hose down in the dipstick hole, one hand to keep the discharge hose in a container, and two hands to operate the pump."

Often the neoprene hose curled up in the hot oil and thus didn't get all the old oil out. Jim bought a length of ¼-inch galvanized-metal brake tubing and cut the flanges off (see illustration). He boiled the end of the neoprene tube to soften it and then slid it over the metal tube and secured it with a small hose clamp. He tied a 10-inch string 4 inches from the end of the discharge hose with a wire tie. When he changes the oil, he ties the other end of the string to the handle of a gallon milk jug, which won't spill easily. When he finishes pumping oil, he caps the brake tubing with the top of a Bic pen, plugs the end of the discharge hose with another small cap, and carries the pump ashore in a plastic bag—an easy way to convert a four-handed chore to a two-handed snap.

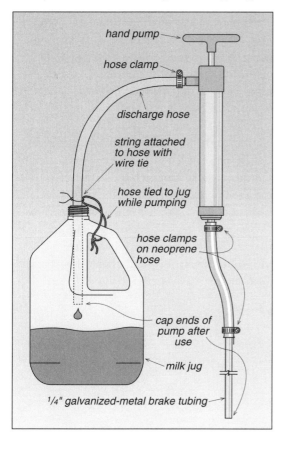

hand pump

hose clamp

discharge hose

string attached to hose with wire tie

hose tied to jug while pumping

hose clamps on neoprene hose

cap ends of pump after use

milk jug

¼" galvanized-metal brake tubing

Oil-change tip

From Dale Wilson of Topeka, Kansas, comes this hint for changing an oil filter on *Trilogy*, his Hunter 34. Place a 1-gallon Ziploc freezer baggie around the filter so that the drips fall into the bag. When finished with the oil change, zip the bag shut and dispose of it properly.

Fuel-line washer renewal

Konstantin Kostov recently completed building a 37-foot Bruce Roberts steel sloop, *Helios*. Writing from Zadar, Croatia, he reminds us that while servicing a diesel fuel line, most manufacturers recommend that you replace all copper washers. However, you may not always have replacements on board. If stuck without extra copper washers, heat the old washers to red hot over a stove burner and then douse them in cold water. This treatment softens the metal and ensures that they'll be totally clean. Remembering from my distant past that ferrous metals harden when treated with heat, we asked a metallurgist friend, who confirmed Kostov's assertion. Now if you drop a spare washer into the bilge, you have an alternative to calling for a tow.

Eyebolts instead of padeyes

Any time you can make one piece of gear serve two purposes afloat, you come out a winner. Charles Rice of Goldsboro, North Carolina, needed a strong point to which he could secure a safety-harness tether just outside the companionway of his pocket cruiser. He considered through-bolting a padeye at each side of the companionway. At the same time, he realized he needed a strong point inside the cabin to which he could secure the large icechest that also serves as the cabin step and an occasional seat.

To save the cost and installation time, he combined the two necessities. He installed stainless-steel eyebolts with eye nuts through the cabin back, using a large-diameter washer for backing on each side of the bulkhead. Instead of having to drill three holes each for two separate sets of padeyes, he had one hole to drill and one eye nut to thread into place for an inside/outside attachment of exceptional strength.

Freshwater flush

Auxiliary-engine cooling problems are commonly caused by failed impellers or corrosion in the heat exchanger. Sailors who use their boats sporadically may benefit from this ingenious flushing system suggested by W.M. Wochos of Redondo Beach, California, who sails *Doc,* a custom 53-foot ULDB. Wochos installed a T in the galley-sink drain hose and another in the engine's saltwater intake hose. He connected the Ts with a length of properly rated cooling-water hose and installed a shut-off valve in the new hose (see illustration). To flush, he closes the engine's raw-water intake seacock and the sink-drain seacock. He opens the valve in the new hose to allow water from the galley sink to flow into the engine. W.M. puts a few gallons of fresh water in the sink (he adds several caps of dishwashing soap; check with your engine manufacturer to see if soap is recommended) and runs the engine for about 2 minutes (he waits for soap bubbles to appear in the discharge).

W.M. says that because fresh water is lighter than salt water, it may not be necessary to close the raw-water intake seacock while flushing. From a *Red Shoes* perspective, there are a couple of things to keep in mind. First, the shut-off valve admitting fresh water to the engine should be closed (after flushing)

while there is still water left in the sink, as airlock may occur in the raw-water intake and inhibit incoming water. You should always monitor the raw-water exhaust emissions when starting the engine. Second, the inconvenience of accessing seacocks and valves may discourage habitual use, so keep at it!

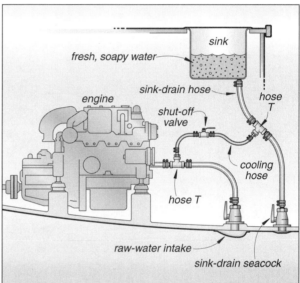

.Cutless bearing

J.R. Downing, who sails his Nimble 30, *Dove,* on the Great Lakes, needed to replace his boat's cutless bearing but found removing the propeller shaft too difficult. Instead, he came

cut four 6-inch lengths of ¼-inch-by-1½-inch steel bar stock and drilled four holes for the bolts used to clamp them to the shaft (see illustration). He then assembled the device as shown.

Be sure that any set screw holding the cutless bearing is loosened or removed before attempting to remove the cutless bearing. The forward bars can be clamped loosely on the shaft, but the aft bars (which bear on the strut, not the shaft) must be spaced far enough apart so the cutless bearing can slide out between them. Spacers can be bar stock or extra nuts on the two bolts. Use threaded rods as tighteners, as shown in the illustration.

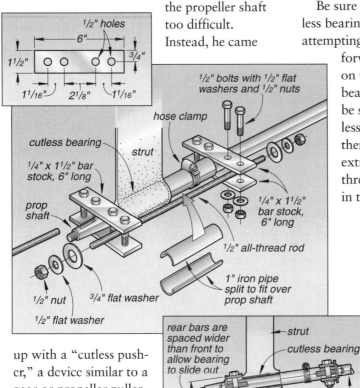

up with a "cutless pusher," a device similar to a gear or propeller puller. He took a length of iron pipe with an inner diameter equal to the diameter of the shaft (1 inch), made it equal to the length of the cutless bearing, and cut it lengthwise. Then he

Prop-shaft packing removal

Anthony Pozsonyi of New York City has discovered a clever way to remove old flax packing from the stuffing box. He suggests straightening out an old fish hook of appropriate size, pushing the hook into the old flax packing and, with a slight twist of the straightened hook, locking the barb onto the fibers and pulling out the old packing.

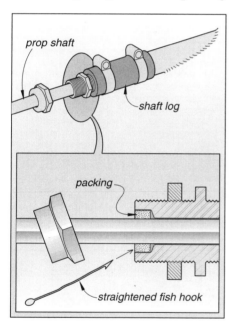

Repacking the shaft gland

When repacking a conventional shaft gland on *Rum Line,* his Gulfstar 37, Edward Manzer of Royal Palm Beach, Florida, wraps the shaft several times with the packing material and slits the wrapped spiral lengthwise along the shaft. That way each circlet is the perfect diameter.

Fluid filler

Jason Halley from Playa Del Rey, California, has found that a hot-water bottle with a hose and a shutoff is the ideal tool for pouring fluids into hard-to-access fillholes. The Perkins 4-107 aboard his boat, *Argo,* is a tight fit, and the very confined space makes pouring oil difficult. He found that using a hot-water bottle permits smooth flow and eliminates mess. The bottle also works to top off transmission fluids, battery water, and coolant reservoirs. Use several hot-water bottles for different fluids or clean one bottle thoroughly between uses to avoid mixing fluids.

Winter Storage

Take cover

This reusable skeleton support for a boat cover (see illustration) comes from Barbara Constans, who keeps her Southern Cross 31, *Tao*, on Lake Michigan. The backbone is

cover from sagging, Barbara strings netting from rib to rib. She says the framework is easy to assemble and disassemble, stores well, and is inexpensive.

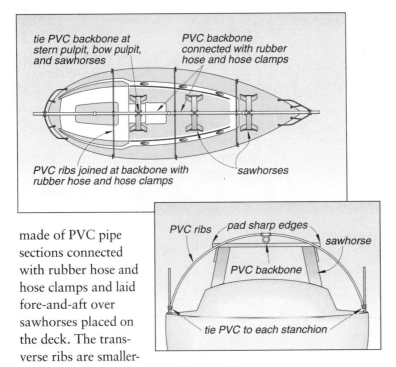

tie PVC backbone at stern pulpit, bow pulpit, and sawhorses

PVC backbone connected with rubber hose and hose clamps

PVC ribs joined at backbone with rubber hose and hose clamps

sawhorses

PVC ribs   pad sharp edges   sawhorse

PVC backbone

tie PVC to each stanchion

made of PVC pipe sections connected with rubber hose and hose clamps and laid fore-and-aft over sawhorses placed on the deck. The transverse ribs are smaller-diameter PVC-pipe sections that are also connected with rubber hose and hose clamps. The ribs are bent over the backbone and tied to the stanchions at the deck. To keep the

Improved tie-downs

Woody Schwartz of Palm Harbor, Florida, sails a 16-foot Chrysler named *Tonic*. His boat's original trailer tie-down strap had a buckle that was difficult to operate and release. He replaced the offending buckle with an automotive-type seatbelt buckle he found at a junkyard. To fasten, he slacks off the seat belt, snaps the buckle together, and pulls the strap tight.

Adjustable tie-downs

Orin Main of Fernandina Beach, Florida, got tired of never having the right length of spare line around for tying this or that aboard his 50-foot Alden ketch, *Tahoma*. He cut line in 6-foot lengths and spliced eyes at each end. The lines can be easily coupled together to provide line of any length. The line-assembly procedure is simple. Take the eyesplice of one line and slip it through the eyesplice of a second line. Then pass the entire length of the first line through its own eyesplice and tighten. Repeat these steps for each segment added. The line can be quickly adjusted to any length, and the splicing, says Main, is a great winter project.

Long-lasting tie-downs

Raymond Weber claims that his boat's canvas cockpit tarp, now more than 10 years old, has outlasted at least five of the poly tarps he'd previously used to cover his Catalina 30 for the winter. "The weakest part of a poly tarp," says Weber, "is at the grommets. It takes only one good gale to pull out the grommets and render the cover useless." Weber remembered a trick used on tents from his Boy Scout days. Selecting a spot near the edge of the tarp, he takes an old tennis or racquet ball and gathers the tarp around it. Then, using a tie-down line, he secures the ball in place with two wraps and two half-hitches drawn up tight. Weber claims that "this kind of tie-down point is so durable it will last longer than the rest of the tarp."

Tie-down quickie

If your boat has a full or modified fin keel, James Fetters's idea for securing a boat cover during seasonal haulouts might work for you. Rather than tying the cover off to the adjustable screwjacks that most boatyards use to support a boat, Fetters installed screw eyes in the wooden blocks that support the keel. Tying the cover off to these eyes eliminates the need to run the cover lines under the keel to the other side of the boat. Fetters sails *Cricket,* a Tartan 37, out of Old Lyme, Connecticut.

Furler protection

An interesting problem and inventive solution comes our way from Cathy and Nick Carlozzi of Cedar Grove, New Jersey. They store their Wauquiez 38, *Merlin,* near Staten Island and noticed that the polluted air was pitting their mast and roller-furling unit. To protect the forestay and roller-furler inexpensively, they placed a strip of plastic dry-cleaning bags—they come in a continuous strip—over the forestay and furler, wrapped it tightly, and secured it every few feet with duct tape.

No more frozen water lines

Proper winterization is a chore, and anything that makes it easier is welcome. Consider this from Shellman Brown of Hyde Park, New York, who owns a Freedom 40. To winterize

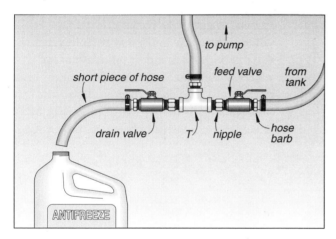

water lines and pumps, Shellman installed a T fitting on the supply side of each pump (illustration below). Two plastic ball valves are connected to the T (all sizes are nominal ¾-inch pipe thread). Normally, the feed valve from the tank is open, the drain is closed, and the pump draws water from the tank. To winterize, insert a short piece of hose from the drain side into a jug of antifreeze. Close the feed valve and open the drain valve, and the pump will take antifreeze from the jug. Keep pumping until the antifreeze comes

through the line, and—presto—you've got antifreeze in the pump and the line and used very little antifreeze.

Fluid control

Kip Bodi of Laurel Hollow, New York, added a sillcock fitting to a plastic bucket to help winterize his boat engine and to control the flow of fluids into the engine from the cockpit. This set-up also solves the problem of trying to get gravity working for you with a siphon and avoids the sloshing of antifreeze and other fluids into the bilge. He simply attaches a hose to the sillcock and leads the hose down to the engine's raw-water intake hose. Water from a garden hose fills the bucket in the cockpit, overflow exits the cockpit drain, and fresh water flushes the raw-water system.

Once the flushing process is complete, he uses the bucket to add the recommended amount of antifreeze to the heat-exchanger system. The entire apparatus costs less than $10 to build. Bodi finds it quite useful for winterization and commissioning work. This mechanism can also be used to recapture environmentally destructive antifreeze prior to launching, which can be saved and reused next season.

5-gallon
bucket

sillcock

hose to engine

MODIFICATIONS AND INSTALLATIONS

This section is a potpourri of solutions, some of which are general, others of which apply only to smaller sailboats. Nancy and I found some of the latter ingenious and wished we'd known of them when we made our 14-month, 26,000-mile trailersailer cruise aboard numerous boats—a cruise that took us from Moosehead Lake in Maine to the Gulf of California, and from Arizona's sizzle to Great Slave Lake's chill in the Northwest Territories of Canada. For example, biting bugs often chased us below at dusk, where we fiddled with a companionway screen that kept most out but always let a few voracious specimens in. In the pages to come you'll find two ideas for companionway screens that really work.

On our trailerable we usually cooked and ate in the cockpit in good weather and would have welcomed the following four ideas for a cockpit table. Of course, each idea that adds convenience also brings a problem—where to stow it—so you'll find that at least a dozen ideas include suggestions that also cover stowing.

Nancy and I welcomed birds and kept a log of the ones we saw, but we often discussed forming our own anti-defecation league. Mostly we objected to the swallows that soiled our sail cover, to the seagulls that bombed our decks from the spreaders (we were grateful that bald eagles were too shy or too polite to add to our burden). So for those who'd rather spend time sailing than cleaning up, we've included six practical ideas that are strictly for the birds, any one of which will cut down on avian calling cards.

I use the same socket wrench set on *Red Shoes* that I took along on *Sea Foam* 25 years ago. Whatever case they came in has long gone, so the sockets have ended up living in a plastic Ziploc baggie that has to be dumped out each time I'm looking for a specific size. Sailor Dick Cartelli came up with an easily made socket organizer using acetone and a piece of foam insulation, an idea that takes the fumbling out of finding the right socket. And then there are the simple why-didn't-I-think-of-that ideas, such as a color-coded method of matching the proper wires when installing spare pumps or fans (neither works properly when wired backwards). Or a device made with lock washers that allows for easy adjustment of fender lines. So whether you're looking for a particular solution or merely reading to enjoy the inventiveness of fellow sailors, the section to follow is a rich vein to be mined for both usefulness and pleasure.

Electronics/ Electrical

Hinged instrument panel

Instead of mounting instruments on the bulk-head or doghouse of his Hunter 26.5, *Le Grand Bleu,* Richard Weinberg built a hinged panel that mounts on the side of the compan-ionway (see illustration). The rectangular ¾-inch piece of wood is ½-inch wider than his instruments and can be flipped out for cock-pit viewing or in to see the displays from below. It also makes removing the instru-ments for theft protection easy. Richard sails out of Casco Bay, Maine.

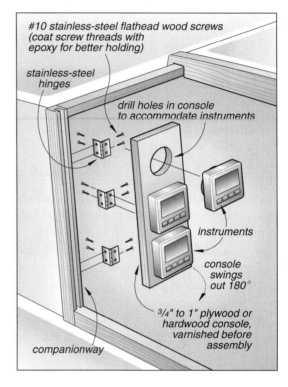

#10 stainless-steel flathead wood screws (coat screw threads with epoxy for better holding)

stainless-steel hinges

drill holes in console to accommodate instruments

instruments

console swings out 180°

¾" to 1" plywood or hardwood console, varnished before assembly

companionway

Water-resistant GPS

Adam Canalungo of Pasadena, Maryland, likes to have his GPS keyboard and display unit mounted in the cockpit of his Gulf Pilot-house 29, *Lively Lady,* but he doesn't trust the water-resistant case to keep out rain and spray. To make the unit more seaworthy, he slips a sealable clear-plastic bag over the unit and punches holes in the bag for the power and antenna cords. The bag protects the unit from spray, while allowing it to operate normally.

Handy GPS and speaker mount

When racing his J/92, *Poohsticks,* off the coast of his native Nova Scotia, Colin Mann uses GPS in fog and bad weather to locate marks and pick downwind gybing angles. He also has to monitor the VHF to listen to identification of premature starters. Rather than send someone below to monitor the speaker or to enter a new waypoint on the GPS, Colin devised a companionway installation to be used during races. He cut a piece of Lexan, using the bottom companionway hatchboard as a template, and mounted his waterproof GPS and VHF speaker on it. He packaged the wires tidily in a flexible-plastic conduit. Instead of unmounting the instruments each time, he stows them below on a grooved, teak holder below.

Compass corruption

This is not exactly a Thing That Works—rather a caution against a Thing That Does Not. Virginian Bruce Hanshaw, the skipper of *Sequoyah,* a Freedom 32, warns of introducing compass error by storing a hand-held VHF too close to the binnacle. The magnet in the speaker, small and weak as it is, can definitely deflect the compass. We learned about compass corruption back in the '70s when they were still making steel beer cans.

Cockpit VHF audio

On *Dear Prudence,* a Catalina 22, Greg Cahamin of St. Petersburg, Florida, uses a clip-on minispeaker to listen to his VHF radio while in the cockpit. When not in use, the minispeaker is clipped to the radio below. Cahamin purchased his unit at Radio Shack; they can also be found at West Marine.

Taming the through-hull geyser

Quentin Kinderman, who sails *Claire-buoyant,* a Pearson 36, out of Edgewater, Maryland, has a revolutionary way to avoid the flood that occurs when a knotmeter transducer or impeller is removed while the boat's in the water. Quentin secures a length of bicycle inner tube over the through-hull with a hose clamp (the tube should be long enough so the end is above the waterline). He moves the transducer up and out of the tube and secures the opening of the tube with a sturdy clothespin while working on the transducer.

On *Red Shoes* we might use dish soap as a lubricant. Even so, we wonder if we could push the transducer back through the tube. But, heck, if a boa constrictor can swallow a chicken...

Avoid through-hull drilling

Bruce Fallert of Fort Myers, Florida, found an easy way to internally mount a depthsounder transducer to the hull of his 26-foot Marie/Holm Folkboat, *Spirit Level,* without through-hull drilling. He took a plumber's PVC pipe-reducer fitting and shaped it to fit the inside curve of the boat's hull. Then he glued the pipe fitting to the inside of the hull with a silicone sealant to form a watertight seal. Next he drilled a small hole in the shoulder of the fitting so he could later fill the gap between hull and transducer with water. Finally, he glued the transducer to the pipe fitting and filled the fitting with water. The water keeps an air-tight, liquid contact between the inside of the hull and the transducer, allowing the unit to function without drilling a hole in the hull.

To shape the PVC pipe fitting, Bruce used a

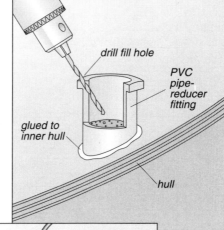

drill fill hole

PVC pipe-reducer fitting

glued to inner hull

hull

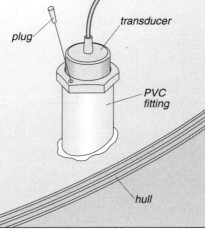

plug

transducer

PVC fitting

hull

cabinetmaker's curve, an angle finder, and a level (to ensure upright mounting of the transducer). He dyed the water with a few drops of food coloring to monitor for leaks. After filling, he covered the drilled hole with a rubber plug so he could top off the water if evaporation occurred. (He hasn't needed to refill it in two years.)

Two factors need to be considered. Be sure to place the pipe fitting over solid laminate, not cored portions of the hull. A transducer won't read through air in the core construction. Also, water could present a problem in freezing temperatures and should be drained if there is a chance of freezing.

Solar-panel mount

Conrad and Charlotte Skladal of Sunnyvale, California, who sailed to East Africa on *Wisp*, found a place to mount a solar panel that is not only out of the way but also well placed to catch the sun's rays.

They replaced the top lifeline wire between the aft lifeline stanchion and the stern pulpit with a 1-inch-diameter stainless-steel tube. To attach the tube, a hole the size of the stan-chion post was drilled in one end so it slipped over the stanchion. It was then secured with a clevis pin. The other end of the tube was notched to slide over the part of the stern pul-pit that secured the original lifeline.

A clevis pin also secured this connection. The solar panel was then mounted on a piece of ½-inch plywood (check your solar panel owner's manual for mounting instructions) that had the ends angled as shown. Two U-bolts were used to clamp the plywood board to the stainless-steel tube. The use of a wing nut and a lock nut on each bolt allowed the clamps to be eased so that the panel could be rotated to face the sun.

To lead the wire from the panel to the house batteries, the Skladals used a short conduit of ½-inch copper tube that leads to a ⅜-inch pipe-compression fitting. The pipe fitting is tapped into the fiberglass deck and installed with sili-cone sealant to make an inexpensive, water-proof, through-deck installation.

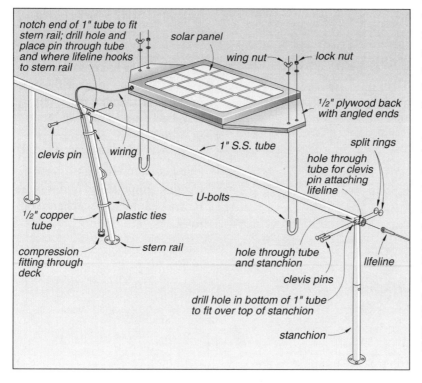

notch end of 1" tube to fit stern rail; drill hole and place pin through tube and where lifeline hooks to stern rail

solar panel

wing nut — lock nut

clevis pin

wiring

½" plywood back with angled ends

1" S.S. tube

split rings

hole through tube for clevis pin attaching lifeline

½" copper tube

plastic ties

U-bolts

compression fitting through deck

stern rail

hole through tube and stanchion

lifeline

clevis pins

drill hole in bottom of 1" tube to fit over top of stanchion

stanchion

Simple wire-leading

M. Tompkins of Oklahoma City, Oklahoma, has a simple way to snake wires through tight confines.

To run small electrical wires through a narrow space between two surfaces (above the headliner, for instance), try using an old steel measuring tape. First, cut off the riveted tip of the tape (and the tape measure's pull tab), so you have a smooth piece of tape measure without any sharp edges or barbs. Then cut a small slice in the tape into which you can wedge a piece of string or fishing line. The string will act as the feeder line for re-running the wire.

Next, carefully feed the tape from the rolled-up spool between the two surfaces. The rigid tape will turn corners with ease. Then tie the wire to the string and pull it through.

Spare-pump wiring

With six pumps on *Rum Line,* his Gulfstar 37, Edward Manzer of Royal Palm Beach, Florida, keeps a spare pump as well as a rebuild kit on board. For ease of replacement, all his pumps are wired the same way—with insulated connectors made by 3M. One lead uses the female part, the other the negative, so hooking them up backwards is impossible.

Protect your pump

Michael Beerli of Sarasota, Florida, has a solution for the irritating problem of a pressurized-water system that continues to run after the tank is empty. Very often the sound of the pump can't be heard over engine noise or by those on deck, and many pumps are damaged by prolonged running without water.

A small indicator light can be installed in the pump circuit so that any time the system is activated, the light illuminates. A 12-volt-DC red, blue, or green pilot light, available at electronic and automotive stores, works nicely. Simply wire the light in parallel to and between the pressure switch and the pump motor.

Autopilot case

Bill Grabenstetter of Rochester, New York, has adapted a length of vinyl drain gutter to serve as a case for his tiller autopilot unit. He cut two pieces of gutter just longer than the autopilot and attached the two pieces with a long, brass piano hinge. Teak trim strips down the length of the gutter pieces add lateral support to the box. Foam padding, cut to fit the autopilot and glued into the new box, keeps the unit snug. "Most autopilots are quite rugged, but this case provides enough extra protection that I now store my autopilot in a cockpit-seat locker instead of somewhere below out of reach," said Bill. The total cost was around $10.

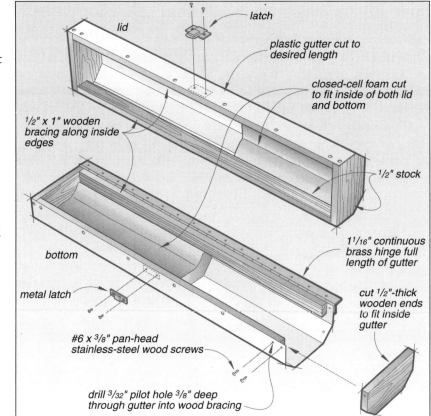

lid

latch

plastic gutter cut to desired length

closed-cell foam cut to fit inside of both lid and bottom

$1/2$" x 1" wooden bracing along inside edges

$1/2$" stock

$1 1/16$" continuous brass hinge full length of gutter

bottom

metal latch

cut $1/2$"-thick wooden ends to fit inside gutter

#6 x $3/8$" pan-head stainless-steel wood screws

drill $3/32$" pilot hole $3/8$" deep through gutter into wood bracing

Mobile radar mount

While aboard Earl Gill and Barbara Malone's *Sonnet,* we saw that their radar display was mounted on a T-track fastened on the headliner. Similar to track lighting, the display can slide from the nav station to the companionway, where it swivels 180 degrees so the helmsperson can see it. Earl mounted slides on the radar set for the T-track and bundled the power and antenna lines together. When the display is at the nav station, Earl hangs the bundled wires on a hook; when the display slides over to the companionway, the wires are taut along the headliner, high and out of the way. Supporting the set in this way, Earl says, also freed up considerable space in the nav station.

VHF holder

A hand-held VHF is useful, but keeping it at hand and secure in the cockpit can be a challenge. Chuck Coykendale, a catboat sailor from Ohio, solved this problem by making a wooden holder out of a 3½-inch-by-3½-inch-by-1½-inch piece of wood (teak might be best). Chuck used a drill and chisel to hollow out a slot in the block that's equal to the dimensions of the base of his VHF.

The block can be mounted almost anywhere in the cockpit, and when not in use the VHF fits snugly into the block. I can see the usefulness of this holder, particularly for buddy-boaters. When your buddy wants to chat, the VHF is usually below, and the last thing you want to do is leave the helm. A holder like this mounted to the binnacle platform would be most convenient.

Breaker breaker

A neat solution to the problem of a crowded breaker panel was sent to us by Jim Hackney. The light for his cockpit-mounted compass was wired to the running-light switch. His boat, *Gaviota Tu,* a Pacific Seacraft Crealock 34, also has a tricolor at the masthead for use under sail. When the boat was sailed at night, Jim used the tricolor, which meant that the compass light wasn't on.

His solution was to incorporate diodes (the equivalent of one-way streets for electricity) in two places. The first is between the running-light switch and the compass-light wire; the second is between the tricolor switch and the compass-light wire. This ensures that the compass light has power when either switch is activated; the diodes prevent the running-light switch from affecting the tricolor switch and vice-versa.

Diskette rehab

Aboard *Red Shoes*, Nancy and I recently faced an epic disaster. All my 3½-inch computer diskettes (stored in a cool place, but still in their cardboard boxes) had developed mold, making them unreadable. Lost data included book manuscripts, articles, tax records, journals, letters, and irreplaceable addresses. Furthermore, each time I tried to read a corrupted disk, the mold messed up the computer drive. I dampened (not soaked) two wads of cotton with isopropyl alcohol. Then I opened the metal slider and held the cotton gently against each side of the inner disk while I spun the diskette with a screwdriver. Having also cleaned the computer drive with a cleaning kit, I made the dirty diskettes regurgitate every byte.

We now store diskettes in tightly closing Tupperware containers with bags of silica gel. (Note: A call to 3M told me that some diskettes will react poorly to alcohol. It may be best to take the plastic disk housing apart, clean the disk with a solution of warm water and a mild detergent, and then put the cleaned disk into a new plastic housing. To get a new housing, you must take apart a new diskette, but your diskette full of data is probably worth it.)

More cockpit space for tiller boats

A problem with tiller steering is the tiller's arc, which takes up a lot of cockpit space while under way. Rex Rexrode, who sails his Watkins 25 out of Palm Bay, Florida, made an 18-inch tiller for his autopilot out of ¼-inch aluminum plate and bolted it to the rudderstock (see illustration). While sailing with the autopilot, Rexrode can raise the 5-foot main tiller to clear space in the cockpit but can get to it quickly in an emergency. The autopilot tiller is out of the way when the boat is hand-steered.

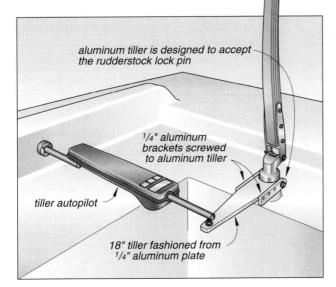

aluminum tiller is designed to accept the rudderstock lock pin

¼" aluminum brackets screwed to aluminum tiller

tiller autopilot

18" tiller fashioned from ¼" aluminum plate

Ground Tackle/Docking

Homemade flopper stopper

A flopper stopper can bring relief in a rolly anchorage where the boat heels one way before the wind or current and large swells roll in from another direction. Evan Gatehouse, who sails *Ceilydh,* a Fortune 30 cutter, lost patience with his rolling boat while anchored off Santa Barbara. Armed with scrap plywood, line, and a small anchor, he made a roll-damping device that works as long as the lines are adjusted properly (see illustration).

The contraption flutters easily down into the water as the boat rolls toward it, but strongly resists a roll in the opposite direction. "The flopper stopper works best when hung off the end of the boom or a long spinnaker pole, which should be controlled with a preventer(s) and supported by a substantial topping lift," say Gatehouse. He has also hung the device from the bow in a situation where there was uncomfortable pitching (but don't forget it's there).

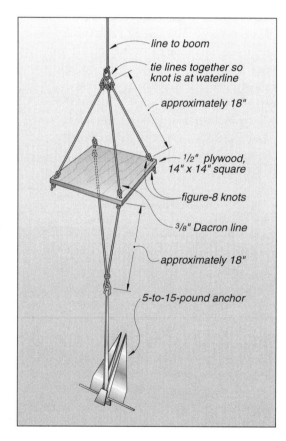

line to boom

tie lines together so knot is at waterline

approximately 18"

$\frac{1}{2}$" plywood, 14" x 14" square

figure-8 knots

$\frac{3}{8}$" Dacron line

approximately 18"

5-to-15-pound anchor

Milk-crate stairs

To make it easier for guests to deal with the high freeboard of *Bear Trap*, a Bristol 440 out of Palm Beach Gardens, Florida, Mike Goldenberg put together six stackable plastic storage crates with stainless-steel seizing wire. Three scraps of exterior-grade plywood attached to the upended bottoms of the crates serve as treads. Remnants of nylon carpeting give the steps a pleasing and cohesive look. Boats with less freeboard will, of course, require fewer steps, but isn't it a crate idea?

Chafing protection

From Mark Davis from Long Island, New York, skipper of the 19-foot O'Day *Kit,* reminds us that fire hose is one of the best materials available for chafing gear. It can also be used along the side of a dock. Used or damaged fire hose is often available from your local fire department, and most chiefs wish we sailors would hurry up and claim it.

More anchor light

A good idea for a crowded anchorage comes from Cliff Bishop, who uses a fluorescent trouble light as an anchor light on his 26-foot Thunderbird sloop. Cliff, who sails out of Bellflower, California, claims it lights up not only his deck, but also a good part of the anchorage. Best of all, it draws only .67 amp at 12 volts.

Controlling your anchor buoy

In order to have his anchor buoy ride as close to the vertical from the set anchor as possible, skipper Steve Christensen equipped *Rag Doll*, his Ericson 38, with a buoy tether that can be adjusted for various depths. He uses a 5-inch-by-20-inch dock fender with a circle of reflective tape as a buoy so it can be located easily with a flashlight. To the bottom of the fender he attached a 1-pound weight to keep the fender floating upright (he warns that you may need to experiment with the weight).

Also attached to the bottom of the fender is a 3-inch stainless-steel snap hook, which is hooked to 35 feet of ¼-inch three-strand line. The other end is tied to the anchor. The line has 3-inch loops tied every 5 feet, each marked with the distance to the anchor (he used a small piece of Tyvek threaded through the line). Ten feet above the anchor Steve tied a small, 3-inch pool float to keep the excess rode from snagging on the anchor or the bottom. The last step

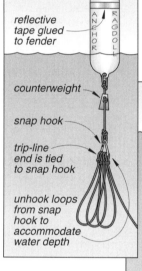

fender

reflective tape glued to fender

ANCHOR   RAGDOLL

counterweight

snap hook

trip-line end is tied to snap hook

unhook loops from snap hook to accommodate water depth

was to write his boat's name and "anchor" on the sides of the buoy.

The length of the tether can be adjusted by hooking successive loops into the snap hook until the desired length is achieved. Steve notes that he sails in the Great Lakes and doesn't deal with tidal ranges. He admits that while his system is quite complex (compared to 40 feet of line tied to a Clorox bottle), knowing exactly where his anchor is set makes it all worthwhile.

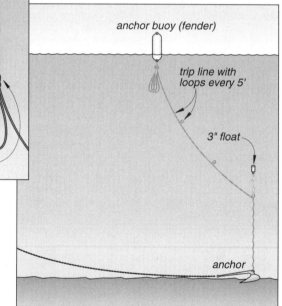

anchor buoy (fender)

trip line with loops every 5'

3" float

anchor

Dockline saver

Vern Barkel of Holland, Michigan, has discovered a way to keep docklines from fraying before their time. He has been tying up to 4-inch-diameter steel pilings for the past few years, causing fraying to be more rapid than on less-abrasive wooden pilings.

His solution begins with cutting the top and bottom off polyvinyl-chloride plastic bottles (windshield and washer fluid), slitting the tubelike leftover portion, and wiring or tying with twine this slippery bearing-like device around the piling. A dockline's sliding and jerking on these piling covers endures a fraction of the abrasion associated with the uncovered piling. A pair of these containers properly lashed together will cover a piling up to a foot in diameter. Lines last a lot longer, and the nearly indestructible bottles are reused prior to recycling, a cost-effective, environmentally sound endeavor.

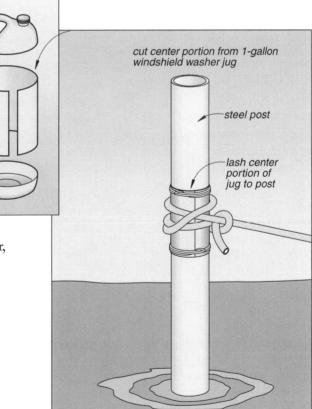

cut center portion from 1-gallon windshield washer jug

steel post

lash center portion of jug to post

Bowsprit protection

If your boat has a bowsprit, as does *Quacker Jacque III,* a Hans Christian 33 owned by Stu and Judy Miller of Marblehead, Massachusetts, this idea might work for you. Their wooden bowsprit was damaged by the anchors they stored there, so they bought two 24-inch stainless-steel rub strakes ($12 each) and screwed them to the bowsprit at the damage-prone areas. The anchors now rest against the strakes.

Chafing gear

For the last five years, Bill Johnson of Seattle, Washington, has used a shippy way to avoid the use of elaborate chafing gear when making fast to barnacle-covered concrete pilings or a rough-surfaced cleat. In each end of a 10-foot length of nylon three-strand line, he spliced a 4-inch eye. On one end he seized the throat of the splice around a thimble. To this he shackles one end of a short (4 to 6 feet) piece of chain. The chain goes around a piling, bollard, or cleat and leads back to the thimble, where a second shackle secures it to the eye. Bill then attaches his docklines to the other eye splice, using a double sheet bend. A bowline would be just as secure but might cause chafe. Also, Bill recommends that both shackles be secured to the thimble in the beginning, as after splicing, parceling, and serving, the line and thimble might be too thick for the shackle mouth to pass over them.

A bridle for chain rode

Dave Wheeler, of Islamorada, Florida, was tired of his boat's chain rode "clunking and grinding" in the bow roller, so he designed a bridle that hooks to the rode and comes back to the port and starboard bow cleats. It not only balances the pull on the ground tackle (as opposed to a single-line snubber from one cleat) and diminishes sailing around at anchor, but also supports the anchor load and silences the chain. To make the snubber, double a length of polypropylene line, and make a small eye with a thimble; attach a chain hook to the eye with a shackle (see illustration). Splice eyes at the two bitter ends large enough to go over the bow cleats. Attach the chain hook onto the top of the chain rode, and let out enough slack in the chain rode so the bridle bears the anchor load. Slack in the rode also helps keep the bridle in place when there's no anchor load.

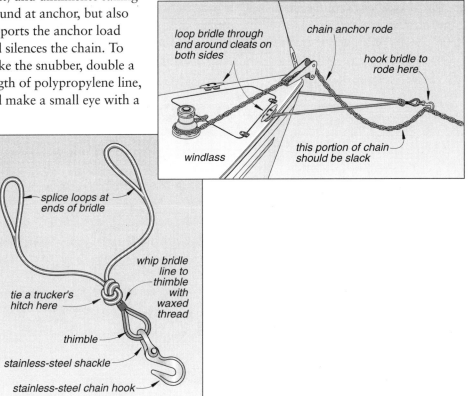

loop bridle through and around cleats on both sides

chain anchor rode

hook bridle to rode here

windlass

this portion of chain should be slack

splice loops at ends of bridle

whip bridle line to thimble with waxed thread

tie a trucker's hitch here

thimble

stainless-steel shackle

stainless-steel chain hook

Anchor-chain stopper

For *Spindrift,* his Catalina 38, David Peffer made an anchor-chain stopper out of a length of vinyl-covered lifeline stock (⅛ stainless-steel wire). He nicropressed a thimble into one end and had a pelican hook swaged to the other. He then shackled the thimble to the padeye in the anchor locker—the same padeye that's also used to tie off the bitter end of the rode. He fine-tunes the length of the chain stopper with the threaded adjustment on the pelican hook.

Fender rig

When we pull up to a new-to-us marina dock, often as not we guess wrong as to proper fender height. Tibor Schimek of Ontario, Canada, tells us how to rig fenders so that they can be speedily adjusted. He says to interlock two stainless-steel spring washers (½ inch to ⅝ inch for ⅛-inch-diameter line) and pull the fender pennant through them as shown. To hold the washers on the line, tie a stopper knot at the end of the line. You can also use this arrangement with shockcords. The price of this modification is a miserly $.50.

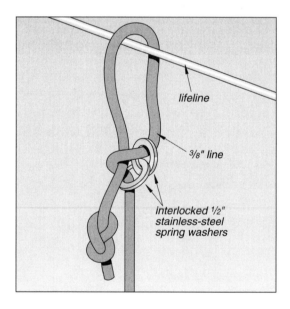

lifeline

3/8" line

interlocked 1/2"
stainless-steel
spring washers

Building a fender board

Craig Holmes of Yarmouth Port, Massachusetts, offers instructions for a fender board that you can build for under $10. Just follow these simple steps.

1. The length of the board you'll need depends on the curve of the hull and the diameter of the fenders. The sharper the hull curve and the thinner the fenders, the shorter the board must be. Holmes used a 5-foot, 6-inch piece of two-by-four for his fender board and secured it to 8-inch-by-23-inch fenders.

2. For the support lines, drill two 4-inch holes through the 4-inch width of the board, one approximately 6 inches from each end.

3. To make the lines that will support the fender board, you'll need two pieces of $5/16$-inch line approximately 15 inches long; weave an eyesplice at one end of each. Feed the unspliced ends through the holes you've just drilled, and tie a stopper knot at the end (see illustration).

4. Drill two $3/8$-inch holes through the board the short way on either side of the support line at each end. The two holes at each end of the board should be 2 inches closer together than the fender diameter.

5. Widen all four holes on one side of the board with a $5/8$-inch bit to a

depth of about $5/8$ inch—enough to allow a knot to be countersunk flush with the face of the board.

6. Cut two pieces of shockcord approximately 3 inches shorter than the circumference of the fenders. Thread the lines through the two pairs of holes from the back side of the board, and tie stopper knots at the ends. Recess these knots into the countersunk holes (see inset).

7. Hang the board on the outside of two fenders by sliding the support-line eye-splices over the fender lines. Stretch one shockcord loop around each fender. The board will remain secure on the fenders, and you can adjust it for dock height.

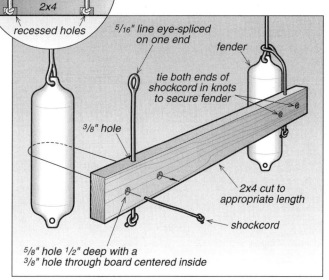

fender
shockcord
2x4
recessed holes

$5/16$" line eye-spliced on one end
fender
tie both ends of shockcord in knots to secure fender
$3/8$" hole
2x4 cut to appropriate length
shockcord
$5/8$" hole $1/2$" deep with a $3/8$" hole through board centered inside

Removable anchor-rode locker

If you dislike smelling a low-tide aroma in the bow, Steve Henkel's removable anchor-rode locker might be just what you're looking for. Steve writes that the permanent anchor-rode locker on his Morgan 24, *Pipit,* which he sails out of Osprey, Florida, quickly accumulated mold, mildew, and smelly marine organisms. He built a small, removable anchor-rode lock-er with three triangular panels of ½-inch marine-grade plywood. The rode locker looks like an upside-down pyramid with an open top and is secured by the V of the hull and two ¾-inch-by-¾-inch battens (see illustration). To remove the locker, Steve lifts it vertically until it clears the battens. He can then take the locker home and hose it down to hospital standards. When the locker is removed, he stuffs a plug of PVC foam into the chain pipe to keep out rain and spray. He asserts that the locker works, because a mud-flat odor no longer invades *Pipit*'s interior.

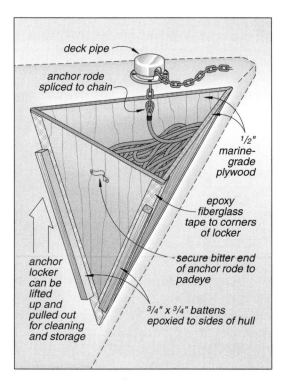

deck pipe

anchor rode spliced to chain

½" marine-grade plywood

epoxy fiberglass tape to corners of locker

secure bitter end of anchor rode to padeye

anchor locker can be lifted up and pulled out for cleaning and storage

³/4" x ³/4" battens epoxied to sides of hull

Efficient ground-tackle storage

As is true on many production boats, the forepeak area divided off for ground tackle in L.J. Ellis's Bristol 32 sloop, *Chelsea,* is far larger than necessary. Ellis created an excellent place to carry spare sails and overnight bags by mounting two U-shaped pieces of pine, held in place against the hull with marine epoxy, halfway forward in the compartment. Removable slats fit into the U grooves; they are cut at different lengths to leave gaps for ventilation and drainage. The slats can be easily removed for cleaning.

An idea that could be incorporated into this forepeak divider to make the space forward of the slat-type bulkhead even more useful comes from Mike Goldenberg of Poslyn Heights, New York. Mike solved the problem of carrying two anchor rodes in the forepeak of his Bristol 40 ketch while keeping them clear of each other. He divided the locker along the centerline using a ¾-inch-thick piece of plywood cut to shape and taped and epoxied in place

(not shown). This divider can be fitted along the centerline, as drainage is provided by the athwartships slats recommended by Ellis.

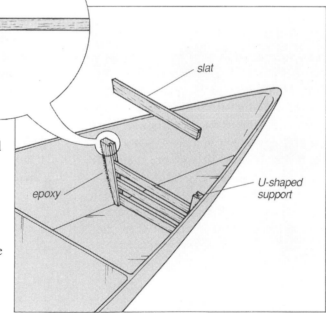

top view

slat

epoxy

U-shaped support

Lunch-hook storage

An idea for smaller sailboats comes from Paul Esterle of Bristol, Tennessee. Because the rode of his grapnel-type lunch-hook anchor tended to tangle in the container (his boat doesn't have a true anchor locker), he purchased a plastic bin large enough to contain the rode and small enough to fit in the stern locker. He secured a small plastic wastebasket to the center of the bin floor with nylon bolts, trimmed the top of the wastebasket to the same height as the top of the bin, and added drain holes. The anchor stores in the wastebasket, and the rode coils neatly around it, secured by the walls of the bin.

Bird barrier

Having returned from vacation to find the mainsail cover on his Newport 20, *Flying Fish,* white with bird droppings, Harvey Garske of Santa Barbara, California, secured a piece of nylon fishing line from the mast to the backstay approximately 4 inches above the boom. The result? No more guano. The boom, of course, must be secured amidships. If your boat has a topping lift, the line can also be secured to it, as the bird barrier will then stay in position no matter where the boom is.

Bird ban(ners)

A funny letter with an amusing but probably impractical idea for most sailors came to us from the pen of Chris Chadwick of Palm Bay, Florida. Here it is, more or less as written: "We keep *Whistler,* our Westsail 32, on a mooring in the Indian River. A flock of sea birds recently discovered her and began roosting on her decks at night. In the morning there wouldn't be one square inch of clean deck. We'd spend hours scrubbing, only to find that the next day our decks were once again covered with droppings. It drove me crazy! I put an owl and rubber snakes on deck—the birds pooped on them. I set out open containers of ammonia hoping the smell would keep them away—they pooped in the containers. In desperation I bought 25 feet of banners at a party store and strung them along the port rail. The next day the decks were again covered with bird dung, with the exception of the port rail. Encouraged, I returned to the party store for more banners, and *Whistler* is now festooned with them. She may look like an open house at a used-car lot, but that's a small price for clean decks."

Aesthetic bird barrier

The war on birds continues. John Walsh of Las Vegas sails out of Cape Cod, Massachusetts, in the summers and takes exception to cumbersome and often unsightly methods for keeping birds from using the spreaders for an MUD (marine unsanitary device). He claims that a thin stainless-steel or bronze wire strung tightly from the shroud to a small padeye on the mast about 6 inches above the spreader keeps birds away. It is almost invisible and also works on multispreader rigs.

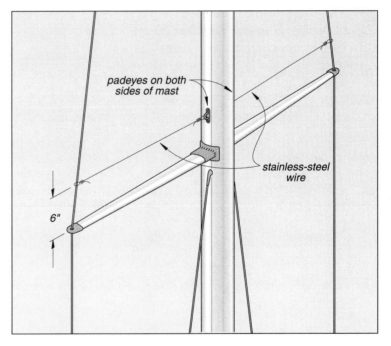

padeyes on both sides of mast

stainless-steel wire

6"

Bird whacker

Dean Coe copes with cormorants and other avian pests intent upon fertilizing the foredeck of his sloop with a trick lacking in aesthetics but brimming with positive effect.

His bird whacker is a 5-foot piece of stiff garden hose clamped and lashed at its midpoint to his jib-halyard shackle, forming a "T" of hose and halyard. He ties a downhaul line to the shackle and raises the halyard to about 10 inches above the spreaders. The downhaul is fastened to the bow pulpit, leaving enough slack so that it can swing but so

that the shackle won't come within 3 or 4 inches of the mast. The hose swings freely from side to side in an unpredictable pattern, making it impossible for the bird to maintain its perch without getting hit. The slightest breeze, wave action, or boat wake sets the device in motion.

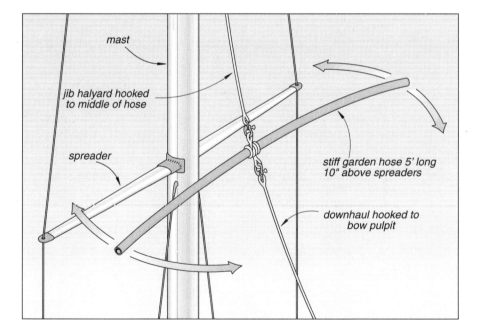

mast

jib halyard hooked
to middle of hose

spreader

stiff garden hose 5' long
10" above spreaders

downhaul hooked to
bow pulpit

Happier birds, clean deck

Bert Jackson of Marathon, Florida, has an idea for how to keep the decks clean. Pelicans and other sea birds used to sit on the pulpit of his son-in-law's CSY 37. "I finally solved the problem by actually providing the birds with a more comfortable resting place: a two-by-four board, approximately 6 feet long, tied athwartships to the top horizontal rung of the bow pulpit and extending out equally to port and starboard." The birds much prefer to land on the board, hence all the "mess" goes overboard.

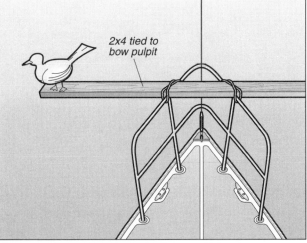

2x4 tied to
bow pulpit

Exterior
Scrub-a-dub-dub

George Reed of Edenton, North Carolina, sails a Nonsuch 30 and finds the bottom scrubber illustrated below to be a competitive aid in local races. "The stiff bristle brushes are very effective when the (buoyant) force supplied by the fender pushes them against the hull. The sailor need only supply the back-and-forth motion and general guidance."

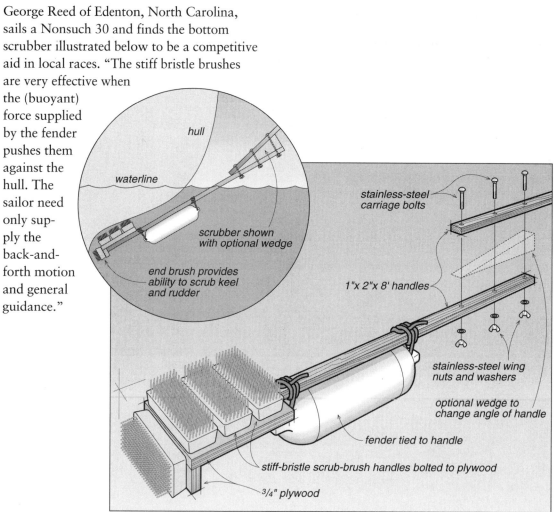

hull

waterline

scrubber shown with optional wedge

end brush provides ability to scrub keel and rudder

stainless-steel carriage bolts

1"x 2"x 8' handles

stainless-steel wing nuts and washers

optional wedge to change angle of handle

fender tied to handle

stiff-bristle scrub-brush handles bolted to plywood

3/4" plywood

Protect your fingers

Lin Pardey writes: "As a mad varnisher I had come to dread the damage sanding did to my fingertips. I tried using masking tape to keep from wearing through my skin. It worked, but the tape was messy if it got wet and left goo behind when I pulled it off. Then I found a product designed for workers in the electronic-assembly business and for jewelers who handle a lot of abrasives.

"Certain types of safety tape are made from rubber (latex)-coated gauze that sticks to itself. It is easy to wrap around your fingers and readily tears into appropriate lengths. It helps you grip tools and sandpaper better and works well when wet. For wet-sanding the bottom of a race boat, for rubbing down varnish work, or for any job with abrasives, this tape is well worth the price of just over $1 a roll.

Hand-sanding tool

Bob Whittier of Duxbury, Massachusetts, believes that there will always be a need for handsanding to give the delicate touch necessary in corners, grooves, and rounded spots. Hard-rubber sanding blocks aren't always appropriate because of their rigid structure. Abrasive paper wrapped around a standard blackboard eraser, available in any office-supply store, makes a versatile sanding tool. It will readily conform to many of the curved surfaces encountered in boat work, yet its rigid backbone makes it easy to hold and manipulate. Pressure is applied uniformly, and better work can be done with little risk of cutting through a fine finish.

Bottom sanding within reach

Sanding your boat's bottom can be extremely tiring, particularly if your boat has a deep draft. Stu and Judy Miller of Marblehead, Massachusetts, have solved the problem when sanding *Quacker Jacque III,* their Hans Christian 33, by using a drywall sandpaper holder. The holder has a padded foam bottom, holds a 12-inch-by-3-inch piece of sandpaper, and has a swivel joint that allows excellent maneuverability. For curvy and difficult places such as around the propeller, they use a sanding block attached to a swab handle. They find sanding a lot easier because of the added reach their be-poled sandpaper provides.

Do-it-yourself custom lettering

Matt Delaney from Abington, Massachusetts, asks if you've ever thought of having the name of your boat made into a graphic design. He claims you can save money by making it yourself. A graphic-arts supply house can sell you the adhesive-backed vinyl (by the foot or roll) in a wide variety of colors, including gold leaf, prisms, and metallics. It will last for years.

Delaney used a design program on his home computer, printed out a full-size pattern, and traced it onto the vinyl. Delaney recommends cutting the vinyl with an X-Acto blade. Delaney used Frisket (a temporary adhesive, available at art-supply stores) to position the letters before removing the backing to firmly adhere the vinyl to the boat.

If vinyl application is new to you, practice with the scrap material left over after cutting out your design. To achieve a professional-looking application, make sure the boat surface is clean (no wax, dirt, or moisture), and rub the vinyl from the center outward to eliminate air bubbles.

Delaney designed the graphics for his Starwind 27, *Marlin,* to look similar to the design in the logo of the boat's model name. The application is in its third year, he says, and looks like it did the day he put it on.

Removing tape

Sam Fiske, who sails *Traveller,* an O'Day 39, out of Osprey, Florida, claims to have great success with removing vinyl or paper tape from all kinds of surfaces. He sets a hairdryer for high heat and holds it 3 to 4 inches from the tape until the heat softens the glue. Sam then uses a putty knife to gently edge and peel off the tape.

Through-the-deck fittings

When installing stanchions and other through-the-deck fittings, careful attention must be given to sealing the fastenings. According to Larry Gonzalez of Plantation, Florida, threads tend to wipe off sealer as they are pressed into a hole. Because of this "wiping" action, leaks occur. To prevent water from seeping down through such fittings, countersink the hole in the deck in order for the sealer (when hardened) to act as an 0-ring. Keep the screw head stationary, and tighten it by turning the nut.

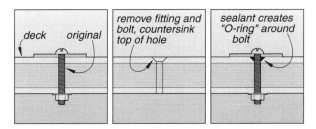

Hatch screen I

Sometimes summer bugs can give you the screening meanies. Bill Cullen, who sails *Panacea,* a Pearson 28, on Tampa Bay, Florida, suggests a companionway hatch screen that's both simple and cheap. At a fabric store, buy nylon netting, a package of grommets, and several feet of light line. At a tackle store, pick up some fishing weights—he recommends at least 15 1-ouncers. Size the netting to cover both the horizontal and vertical parts of the companionway and wide enough to leave an extra 4 inches of material at each side for a hem. Fold the top corners, and install grommets in the doubled fabric. At the bridgedeck end, install three grommets and tie on the fishing weights with thread. Tie the grommets on the upper, horizontal portion to the handrails or any other convenient place. If necessary, secure the sides of the netting with sinkers as well. This approach can be modified for any hatch. Bill finds his system beats the hassle of Velcro and glue.

Hatch screen II

Another means of barring bugs from belowdeck comes from Ted Kline of Miami, Florida. On *Leading Lady,* an Island Packet 31, he replaced his upper two hatchboards with a single piece of ¹/₂-inch plywood, the center of which he cut out and replaced with a screen (see illustration). A companion idea of Ted's is worth mentioning; he installed a sliding bolt to the inside of the hatch so he can lock the boat from the inside when he's sleeping.

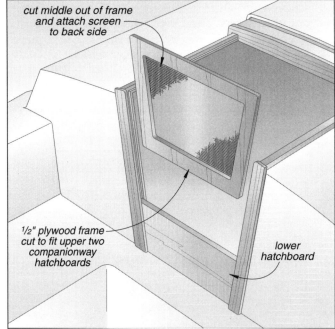

cut middle out of frame and attach screen to back side

¹/₂" plywood frame cut to fit upper two companionway hatchboards

lower hatchboard

Tiller stiller

From Ed Rudetsky of Brooklyn, New York, comes a simple method to immobilize a tiller. It comes in handy while bending over the transom to start the outboard, dropping sails, or ducking below. Rudetsky has a "flip box" that sits underneath his tiller, with holes into which a permanently mounted pin on the underside of his tiller fits. When the box is not in use, he flips it 180 degrees into the cockpit well. Another option is to permanently mount the box, drill a hole through the tiller, and use a stainless-steel pin to lock the tiller at any angle. Rudetsky credits the idea, which he adapted to *Mike and Sam,* his Columbia 22, to his friend Eddie Bastien.

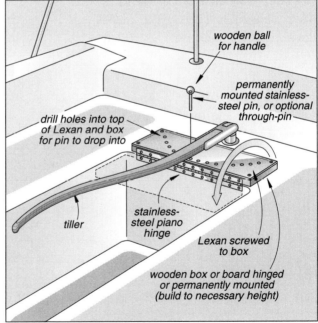

wooden ball
for handle

permanently
mounted stainless-
steel pin, or optional
through-pin

drill holes into top
of Lexan and box
for pin to drop into

tiller

stainless-
steel piano
hinge

Lexan screwed
to box

wooden box or board hinged
or permanently mounted
(build to necessary height)

Tiller extension

J. William Arpin of St. Cloud, Florida, who singlehands his 17-foot catboat, found that his tiller was too short to allow him to move around the cockpit while keeping a hand on the helm. To lengthen the tiller and maintain the traditional look of his boat, he constructed a tiller extension from mahogany (other hardwoods could be used).

Purchase the piece of hardwood of your choice at a local chandlery. (If you have trouble finding the right type of wood, look in the Yellow Pages under "hardwoods" or "wood.") Buy a piece with the same dimensions as your tiller; its length should be three-and-a-half times the distance you would like to extend the tiller.

From the wood you will need to form two coupling pieces, the tiller extension, and two cross braces, which help secure the coupling pieces to the original tiller. To make the cross braces, cut a piece three times the width of your tiller from the new length of wood. Cut this piece in half, lengthwise, to make a pair of cross braces. Cut the remaining piece into thirds.

Clamp the two coupling pieces to the tiller with C clamps, overlapping the end of the tiller by half the length of the coupling. Place the cross braces as shown, and pre-drill the braces and coupling pieces with pilot holes to prevent the wood from splitting when installing wood screws. Attach the couplings and the cross braces to the tiller using wood screws and epoxy.

After the epoxy has cured, slip the tiller extension between the couplings and secure it at the desired length with wood screws and epoxy. Let the epoxy cure, sand the assembly, and varnish it. Consider making a hand grip from lashing twine, a nice cosmetic detail. The result is a classic-looking addition to any boat.

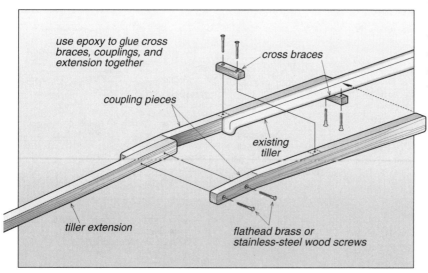

use epoxy to glue cross braces, couplings, and extension together

cross braces

coupling pieces

existing tiller

tiller extension

flathead brass or stainless-steel wood screws

Tiller-extension tamer

David Demilia of Marlton, New Jersey, got tired of fussing with the tiller extension on his Capri 14.2, *Bon Bini*. He didn't like the way it tended to flop around and get in the way when he was seated inboard on a leisurely sail. To keep the tiller extension tucked away when not in use, he installed a plastic clip (meant to hang brooms or other tools) on the outboard end of the tiller. He can now clip the extension to the tiller for daysailing or easily unclip it and hike out.

Lifeline cosmetics

Stuart Shippey sails *Lorelei,* a 27-foot Bavaria 8.2, out of Pensacola, Florida, and offers this idea to spruce up or maintain lifelines. The plastic coating on *Lorelei*'s lifelines chafed at the stanchions, so Stuart installed short lengths (8 to 12 inches) of snap-on plastic shroud cover (available at West Marine) over the lifelines at each stanchion. Be sure to remove the cover periodically and inspect the condition of the lifeline wire, as lifeline failures often occur at the stanchions and/or swage fittings.

Stronger stanchions

By nature, stanchions and pulpits are suscep-
tible to bending and distortion. If yours have
suffered such abuse, or if you want to
strengthen them beforehand to minimize
bending, Skip Allan of Capitola, California,
recommends inserting a dowel or broom handle into the stanchion tube as far as it will go.
"The fit should be snug," he writes, "and per-
suasion can be applied with a rubber mallet.
The added stiffness is substantial; it's a good
idea to add backing plates belowdecks."

Custom stanchion fittings

Tom Flader of Fond du Lac, Wisconsin, has
made a variety of useful devices from PVC
tubing that has the same inside diameter as
the outside diameter of his stanchions and
pulpits. He cuts and removes a lengthwise slit
from the tubing so he can snap the remaining
portion of the tubing securely onto a stanchion or pulpit. The greater the width of the
removed slice, the easier it is to snap the tubing on and off the stanchion. Tom has found
that starting with a small slice and then gradually filing away the edges with a file or plane
makes it easier to adjust the tubing's holding
power.

These fittings can secure many things to
your boat on a temporary "light load" basis.
With countersunk screws driven from the
inside out through the tubing's centerline you
can screw to the tubing whatever you want to
secure to the stanchions or pulpits, such as
small cleats for fenders, a flagstaff, a temporary antenna, and a flashlight holder.

Securing lifelines

When Larry Marvel of Spokane, Washington, bought his San Juan 7.7, the one-piece single lifeline from the bow pulpit to the stern pulpit created problems. When he released the pelican hook to drop the lifeline for boarding, the entire lifeline dropped and the foredeck netting slackened. Not only was this unsafe, but the lifeline was also difficult to stretch back out again.

"I purchased 2¼-inch U-bolts and clamped each one on the lifeline immediately aft of the first stanchion forward of the boarding area on each side of the boat. I then took two 35mm film containers, with the lids attached, and drilled a ⁵⁄₁₆-inch hole through the top and the bottom. I split the canisters on one side down to the holes and slipped them over the U-bolts. Then I covered the canisters with white rigging tape. They are now the same color and diameter as my foam lifeline cover. When I release the lifeline only the cockpit section releases, and there's no more tangled netting on the bow."

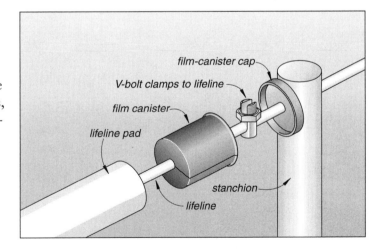

film-canister cap

V-bolt clamps to lifeline

film canister

lifeline pad

stanchion

lifeline

Comfort on the rail

Larry Stephenson has received great reviews since replacing the lifeline in his cockpit with straps made primarily from 2-inch webbing. Two pieces of webbing are sewn together with a length of batten sandwiched inside. The ends are overlapped and sewn around large D-rings. The end result gives you a wide area on which to lean that won't wrinkle or twist and that gives up little of the strength necessary for safety. Now, whether on the leeward rail or just leaning back and relaxing, the safety line doesn't detract from comfort on the rail.

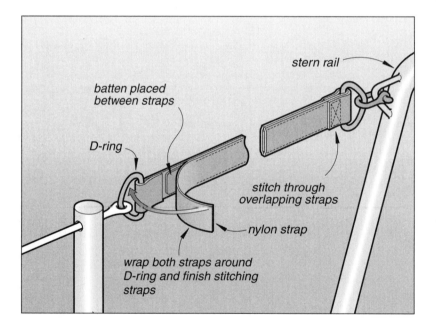

stern rail

batten placed
between straps

D-ring

stitch through
overlapping straps

nylon strap

wrap both straps around
D-ring and finish stitching
straps

Cockpit table I

For *Wind Dreamer,* which is equipped with binnacle wheel steering, Herb Epstein of Boynton Beach, Florida, devised a removable cocktail table. He used pine lumber in 1-inch widths, spaced ¼-inch apart. The table is supported by the spokes of the wheel and a single, hinged leg that folds back and is secured by a Velcro patch for storage. The table is anchored to the wheel spokes with two eyestraps that are mounted to the underside of the table and that have cut-outs big enough to allow them to drop over the spokes. Epstein stained the table and finished it with a satin-sheen varnish.

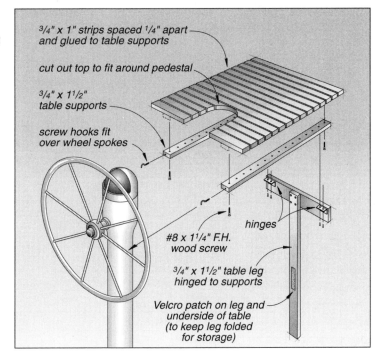

¾" x 1" strips spaced ¼" apart and glued to table supports

cut out top to fit around pedestal

¾" x 1½" table supports

screw hooks fit over wheel spokes

#8 x 1¼" F.H. wood screw

hinges

¾" x 1½" table leg hinged to supports

Velcro patch on leg and underside of table (to keep leg folded for storage)

Cockpit table for boats with tillers

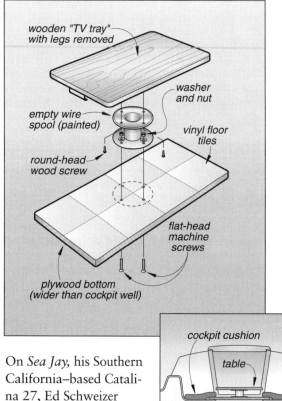

wooden "TV tray" with legs removed

washer and nut

empty wire spool (painted)

vinyl floor tiles

round-head wood screw

flat-head machine screws

plywood bottom (wider than cockpit well)

cockpit cushion

table

cockpit well

the spool and used bolts to secure it to the plywood, which for aesthetic purposes he covered with white-vinyl floor tiles. He then centered the table top on the spool and fastened it with wood screws. The spool separates the table and plywood by about 4 inches, allowing the table to "float" over the cockpit cushions (see illustration). Since the size of the spool dictates height of the table above the cockpit seat, experiment with several spools to get the best table height.

The table can be slid forward or aft. It's worth noting that some TV table–types are made of very thin wood, so you may have to glue a wooden block to the bottom of the table top to achieve sufficient thickness for wood screws. We also suggest painting the wire reel to prevent rust.

On *Sea Jay,* his Southern California–based Catalina 27, Ed Schweizer built the cockpit table shown in the illustration using a wooden TV table–type top (with the legs removed), an empty wire spool, and a piece of plywood slightly wider than his cockpit well.

Ed drilled four holes through each side of

Cockpit/saloon table

Eric Wakely's dual-use table is a beautifully
finished and functional piece that can be used
in the cockpit or the saloon. The table itself
can be any size, but it's the manner of support
that's interesting.

To avoid interfering with the arc of the
tiller on his Cal 28, *Keani Kai,* Eric used two
angled supports made from 7/8-inch stainless-
steel tubing, two 60-degree female fittings,
and two 30-degree fittings on the bulkhead.
Because the forces on the fittings (the bulkhead fittings in particular) are substantial,
Eric strengthened the bulkhead with a plywood backing plate.

Since any protrusion in the cockpit or
main saloon is a possible source of
injury, we recommend covering the fittings with rubber feet (like those used for
crutches) when not in use.

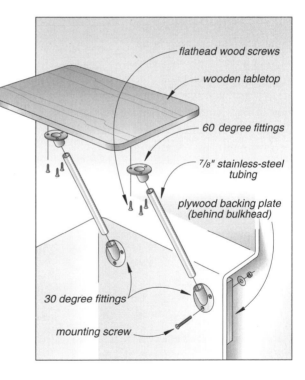

flathead wood screws

wooden tabletop

60 degree fittings

7/8" stainless-steel
tubing

plywood backing plate
(behind bulkhead)

30 degree fittings

mounting screw

Cockpit table II

Like many people who choose tiller steering, Robert Miner of Strongsville, Ohio, wished he could figure out a way to have an easy-to-mount cockpit table. Without a wheel pedestal to which one end of the table can be attached, this presents a problem. Miner designed his own solution, one that shows some careful thought.

He writes, "The table has three legs hinged beneath the tabletop. The front leg flairs at the top to nearly half the width of the table, giving strength to the hinged joints—that is, the single central leg on the forward end provides knee room for easy seating access and folds between the two legs on the aft end for storage. The two aft legs drop into tight-fitting U-shaped brackets mounted high on the forward face of the lazaret or helmsperson's seat. A pin at the bottom of the forward leg drops into a recess in the cockpit sole. This makes the table

quite stable, though some day I'll probably add pins to the bottoms of the aft legs to prevent the little bit of forward movement that is possible there.

"The folded table is 2 inches thick and stores against the empty bulkhead in our

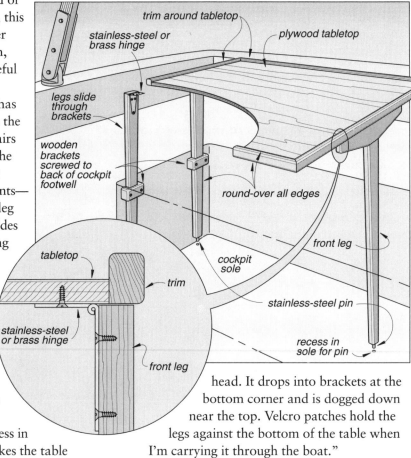

head. It drops into brackets at the bottom corner and is dogged down near the top. Velcro patches hold the legs against the bottom of the table when I'm carrying it through the boat."

Custom-fitted cockpit drink holder

An inexpensive, custom-fitted removable holder for canned drinks was suggested by Jane Piereth of San Rafael, California. To make it, she says, "Trace the shape of the bottom five inches of your companionway board onto a piece of plywood. Cut out the shape and fasten it to a four-hole teak drink holder (available from marine stores and catalogues) by drilling and screwing from behind. No holes need to be drilled in the boat, and the holder is low, so it's easy to step over when you use the companionway. If you leave a half-inch of plywood above the teak holder, it will take the brunt of the abuse if someone does step on it. When the holder is not in use, I stow it upside down at the head of a quarterberth."

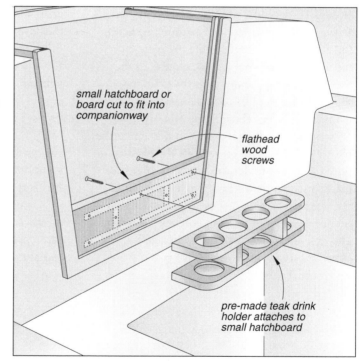

small hatchboard or board cut to fit into companionway

flathead wood screws

pre-made teak drink holder attaches to small hatchboard

More light in the cabin

"Tired of the dark interior of your sailboat when the hatch has to be closed?" asks Joseph O'Flynn of Somers Point, New Jersey. His solution is to install clear flexible plastic over the companionway hatch, much as you might use screening. "Purchase the plastic film at your hardware store. Buy the heaviest gauge you can find." O'Flynn uses self-stick Velcro to hold down the plastic and places the hook half of the Velcro around the perimeter of the hatchway with the hatch closed. Then he attaches the other half of the Velcro to the first, leaving the tape protecting the adhesive in place. He cuts the plastic to the approximate size, leaving excess all the way around. Beginning with the sides, he removes one piece of protective tape at a time from the Velcro, exposing the adhesive, and presses the plastic to the adhesive, keeping the plastic tight. When you remove the plastic, put your finger under the Velcro to prevent tears. You can then trim the plastic around the Velcro. O'Flynn has used his clear hatch on hot days with the air-conditioner running and on cold nights with the heater going. When it's not in use, he rolls it up and stores it in a chart tube.

Polishing Lexan

Jim Scala, who sails *La Scala,* a Hans Christian 43, out of San Francisco, says the following idea works for him. To polish Lexan or flexible dodger windows when they've become dulled by the sun, he scrubs them with a rag and some abrasive toothpaste. "The toothpaste," he says, "should contain baking soda. Toothpaste works because rubbing causes the abrasive particles to become smaller as the polishing continues."

Nancy and I aren't able to test most of the ideas that are printed in this column, but if they are clear, useful, and logical, we accept the contributor's claim that the idea works for him or her. In this case, however, I happened to have thoroughly dulled my watch crystal by spraying it with insect repellent (I know, I know; read the instructions on the can). It's also heavily scratched. So at Scala's suggestion, I got out the Crest and began scrubbing. Impatient, I upgraded to Babbo. Frustrated, I moved on to Brasso. The dullness caused by the repellent was removed after a few applications of toothpaste, but the scratches remained. My watch, however, is radiant and hasn't a trace of halitosis.

Binnacle cover

Tired of replacing fabric compass covers that are destroyed by sun or blown away in strong winds? Jerry Atkinson of Edenton, North Carolina, was. He made a cover by cutting up an old soccer ball. It protects his compass from weather and sun and stows away easily. "During a recent relocation," says Jerry, "the compass cover stayed in place while being trucked at highway speeds." He has used his on *Sea Esta* for the last four years. It seems to me it would offer shock protection for the compass as well.

Cockpit-instrument covers

Emil Gaynor of Camarillo, California, writes, "After a deck ape crushed one of my instrument displays with a winch handle, I decided to add some protection. I made a cover of Plexiglas to fit the instrument and then drilled and countersank three holes for fasteners. I also drilled holes of the same diameter through the instrument flange. The Plexiglas cover can be fastened with bolts, washers, and nuts, or the instrument flange can be tapped for machine screws. The covers aren't sealed to the instruments, so they can easily be removed for cleaning." Don't forget: If you accidentally spray a cover with insect repellent, just get out the toothpaste, and rub, rub, rub...

Instrument-panel protection

Richard Coerse of Alexandria, Virginia, decided to make the instrument panel on his boat less prone to the damage that can be caused by a wayward winch handle, a deck shoe, or the sun. For less than $6, he added a Lexan panel cover with the same screws to mount both the panel and the cover. He then cut out just enough of the Lexan to allow access to the key and starter switch.

He stitched a sun cover of acrylic sail-cover fabric and sandwiched the fabric between the top edges of the Lexan and the panel-mounting flange. He added a couple of snap fasteners below the panel so the acrylic can be rolled down over the Lexan and snapped in place. He rolls up the fabric when he needs to see the instruments. Shaded by the acrylic, his instruments will keep looking new and unfaded for years, and it's unlikely that the glass faces of the oil-pressure and temperature gauges will crack.

With this or any other on-deck key installation, it's imperative that your key switch be waterproof; otherwise, a damp-induced short could burn out your starter motor. Don't assume your switch is waterproof until you check it.

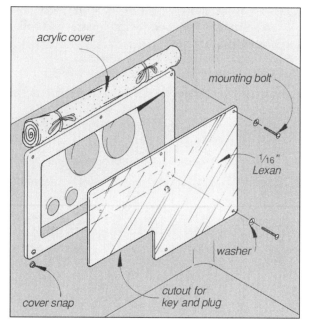

Portlight covers

Alexander Yaxis of Amityville, New York, wrote regarding his concerns about using cloth curtains on teak rods aboard his H-28 ketch. "They're a fire hazard if they are near the galley; they harbor mildew, fade, require careful washing, block out sunlight, and aren't neat or shipshape." His solution: Portlight-shaped translucent ovals of 1/16-inch-thick semiflexible translucent plastic (Polyplastics's Pan-Ion) plus two roundhead screws.

He cut the plastic 1/2-inch larger than the portlight, then notched each end as shown in the figure. Two roundhead wood screws are positioned at each end of the portlight to hold the solid "curtains." To put the

curtains up, he bends the plastic into a curve; it snaps into place. When not in use, the curtains are stowed flat under a bunk cushion. These curtains will work equally well for opening ports as long as the screws are positioned on the opening flange.

For boats with bronze or alloy portlight frames, sheet-metal screws or roundhead machine screws can be used instead of wood screws. Another useful adaptation would be to carry a set of opaque or very dark-colored "curtains" to darken the interior of the boat and help the early-morning off-watch to get a sound sleep.

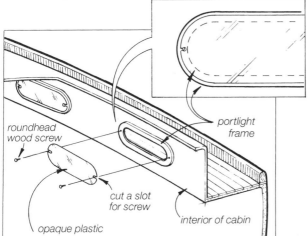

roundhead
wood screw

portlight
frame

cut a slot
for screw

opaque plastic

interior of cabin

Lazaret-lid holder

Lazaret lids tend to fall on your fingers when you're not looking. Florida cruisers Dave and Harriet Havanich solved this problem on *Pageant* by permanently attaching a length of shockcord to one of the ribs that strengthens the lid. A loop on the other end stretches over a winch mounted on the side of the cockpit and holds the lid open. For lazarets without ribs, padeyes affixed with Marine Tex or 3M 5200 will work just fine.

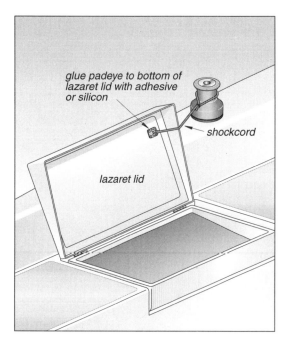

glue padeye to bottom of lazaret lid with adhesive or silicon

shockcord

lazaret lid

Removable cockpit-cushion covers

Ah, where would we be without Velcro? Michael and Tara Crane of Columbia, Missouri, bought a used Cape Dory daysailer, *Freight Train,* with faded and dirty cockpit cushions. Tara, who is finishing a PhD in historic costume and dress, wasn't looking for a recreational sewing job, so she came up with a simple solution that required buying the fabric of their choice in the proper size and a package of iron-on Velcro.

Tara and Michael wrapped each cockpit cushion exactly as if they were wrapping a Christmas present. They attached Velcro where they would have used tape. Now, when the cover gets dirty or the wet dog takes a nap on it, they uncover it, take it home, and throw it in the washing machine. For those who wrap presents as untidily as I do, however, it's best to go for the fitted, sewn covers.

Custom helm seat

Some production boats don't provide a convenient seat for the helmsperson. This was true for Melvin Goldstein on his O'Day 27, *Touché,* on which installing a permanent helm seat would block the diesel engine instrument panel mounted at the aft end of the cockpit. Goldstein built a removable seat that, when it's not in use, can be stored in the cabin. The height of the seat can be adjusted by using boards of different dimensions, and the pine guides stop the

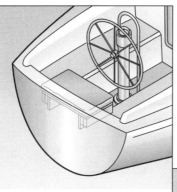

seat from sliding as the boat heels (see illustration).

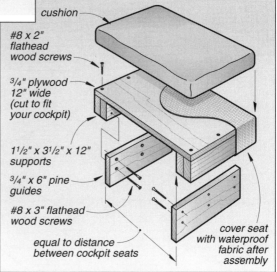

cushion

#8 x 2"
flathead
wood screws

3/4" plywood
12" wide
(cut to fit
your cockpit)

1¹/₂" x 3¹/₂" x 12"
supports

3/4" x 6" pine
guides

#8 x 3" flathead
wood screws

equal to distance
between cockpit seats

cover seat
with waterproof
fabric after
assembly

Under-the-seat stowage

Easy-to-reach, quick-access storage for bulky items you use on deck is difficult to find. Jack Niday, who sails an Ericson 35 out of Balboa Island, California, has attached two pieces of ¾-inch dowel stock lengthwise under his helmsperson's seat as an excellent storage rack for his dock lines. Because the seat is curved and the space inside it is deep, it can accommodate all the necessary lines and keep them tangle free.

On *Puffin,* Doug Schmuck's 28-foot Bristol Channel Cutter, the hatch in the helmsperson's seat is flat and offers only 2 inches or so of storage space. But he found an excellent use for the space. Emergency cable cutters are held against the underside of the hatch by secure quick-release holders, making them readily available.

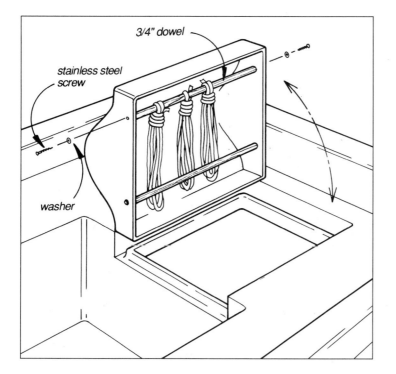

Winch-handle holders

Steve Ackerman of Charleston, South Carolina, wanted to mount winch-handle holders on the steering pedestal of *Paradox,* his Hunter 35.5. To save money and avoid drilling holes in the pedestal, Steve bought two 12-inch sections of 2-inch-diameter PVC tubing. To secure the tubing to the pedestal, he drilled three evenly spaced pairs of holes in each tube. He then strung white-leather boot laces (available from any cobbler) through each pair of holes and tied the tubes to the pedestal. The tube diameter, hole sizes and spacing, and tie-down material can be customized to suit the size of any winch handle.

Stovepipe hat

Although most Charlie Noble (stovepipe) vents are designed to keep out rain, a green wave can defeat them. Donald Launer of Forked River, New Jersey, made a foul-weather cap for the CN vent on *Delphinus,* his 39-foot Lazy Jack schooner, using PVC pipe. A piece of drain pipe, just a bit wider and taller than the vent, is used as a sleeve. One end is capped, and the cap is bonded to the pipe. Donald says, "Originally I'd planned to drill a small hole in the bottom of the PVC sleeve and secure the cap to the boat with a lanyard, but I never did this, and through years of bad weather it has never come off."

Vent restrainers

Snap-in plastic cowl vents can easily fly overboard if they are kicked loose. Emil Gaynor of Camarillo, California, sent in this idea, which he uses on his Cal 2-46. The restraining chain and bar are simple to install. They keep the vent from going overboard but allow it to be removed easily or rotated when necessary.

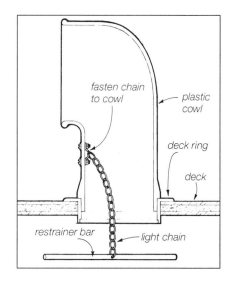

fasten chain to cowl

plastic cowl

deck ring

deck

restrainer bar

light chain

Shock-absorbing padeye

Having had a mainsheet padeye fail from metal fatigue after many years, Shellman Brown of Hyde Park, New York, designed the following shock-absorbing padeye-mount, similar to a motor mount. The device requires two ¹/₂-inch aluminum plates cut as shown. The padeye is drilled and tapped into the upper plate, which is bolted to the lower plate. The lower plate is tapped to receive the machine screws that secure it to the deck (see illustration).

A shock-absorbing patch cut from ¹/₈-inch neoprene is sandwiched between the two plates. The two bolts that bind the plates together are ³/₈ inch, but the holes to receive them are ⁵/₈ inch, and a short length of ⁵/₈-inch (outside diameter) neoprene fuel line is used as a shock-absorbing sleeve. Washers for the bolts are cut from the ¹/₈-inch neoprene sheet. Shellman secures the bolts with nylon lock nuts, which are tightened only enough to remove excess play. He uses a teak block as a spacer between the plates and the deck to allow access to the ³/₈-inch lock nuts and washers.

Brown's padeye has been on the mainsheet for two years, and he recently added one to the mizzen sheet. Although perhaps too fussy for most of us (who might instead install a heavier padeye), Brown's design is sure to please the heart's cockles of skippers who enjoy messing about in boats.

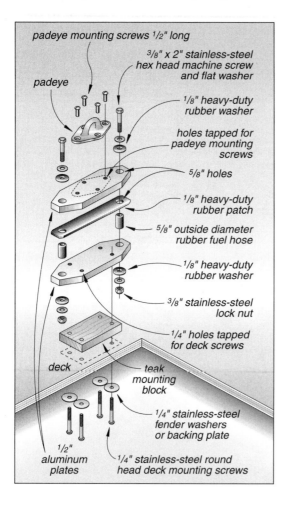

padeye mounting screws ¹/₂" long

³/₈" x 2" stainless-steel hex head machine screw and flat washer

padeye

¹/₈" heavy-duty rubber washer

holes tapped for padeye mounting screws

⁵/₈" holes

¹/₈" heavy-duty rubber patch

⁵/₈" outside diameter rubber fuel hose

¹/₈" heavy-duty rubber washer

³/₈" stainless-steel lock nut

¹/₄" holes tapped for deck screws

deck

teak mounting block

¹/₄" stainless-steel fender washers or backing plate

¹/₂" aluminum plates

¹/₄" stainless-steel round head deck mounting screws

Boom support

Philippe von Hemert of Philadelphia, Pennsylvania, has a good, simple idea for small-boat owners who don't want to install a permanent boom gallows but wish they could sometimes position the boom off-center while in port.

To save guests from hitting their heads as they climb out the companionway on *Chimera,* his 26-foot gaff-rigged sloop, Philippe designed and built an asymmetrical scissors boom support. He used ⁵⁄₄-dimension (1¼-inch) oak and cut the starboard leg of the scissors shorter than the port. As the companionway is about 8 inches off-center to port and his boom rests 8 inches off-center to starboard on the new scissors, the companionway is virtually clear of obstructions. Reversing the support would work, too.

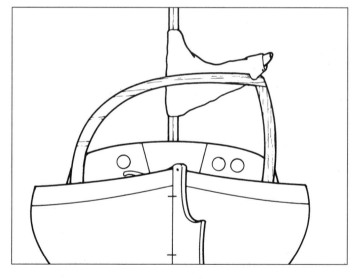

Boom crutch

"We've never felt comfortable with the practice of hanging the boom from the backstay when the mainsail is dropped and furled," write Natalie and Al Levy of Chicago, Illinois. "It would appear to put strain on the rigging, and it is often difficult for short sailors to reach up and clip the boom to the backstay. The swinging boom can make the crew furling the mainsail feel insecure. To make a boom crutch for our 22-foot Ensign, we purchased two ordinary broom handles and cut them down to fit the distance from the cockpit corner to a few inches above boom height. With the two broomsticks crossed to create an X, we drilled a hole and then inserted a bolt, using washers on both sides of the wood. We glued rubber cups meant for orthopedic crutches to the bottoms of the broomsticks to protect the cockpit surfaces. Spread open, the ends fit snugly into the cockpit corners, and the boom rests in the V. With the mainsheet cleated, the boom is secure, and the mainsail is easy to furl.

"You can scale up these sheerleg specs by checking out industrial-style push-broom handles in janitorial supply stores. Foam or felt padding can be glued to the V to protect both boom and crutch, though we have not found this padding necessary."

Inexpensive hand-rail covers

To protect the teak hand-holds and tiller on his O'Day 25, *Phoenician,* Rod Nickel of Merritt Island, Florida, bought 6-foot sections of ¾-inch foam pipe insulation. The insulation has a lengthwise slit and wraps tightly around the teak. To make sure the foam stays in place, Rod advises tying each end of the foam with short lengths of line. Purchased covers for hand-holds tend to be expensive, and they're somewhat complicated for the sew-it-yourselfer to make.

Instant cockpit cover and more

Lin and Larry Pardey carry two multi-purpose canvas cloths, one 4 feet by 6 feet and the other 4 feet by 4 feet, on board *Taleisin*. You can make them from a heavy, white synthetic canvas such as Acrylon, which is not only easy to sew but is less likely to flap in the wind. The cloth should have a 2-inch-wide tabling around all four edges. Corner grommets (either spur tooth or sewn rings) should be firmly secured with extra stitching or webbing to spread the strains. Lengths of ³/₁₆-inch Dacron line should be spliced into each grommet.

The Pardeys use the larger one primarily as an at-sea cockpit cover. The best thing about it, besides its low cost, is that it can be rigged when it's needed and also quickly moved out of the way.

They use the smaller cloth as a simple windscoop when they lie at anchor. It works almost as well as more elaborate scoops and catches wind even if the boat veers 20 degrees to either side of head-to-wind. The lower line is secured below deck. They attach two lines to the upper corner, one led to the spinnaker-pole ring on the front of the mast, 7 feet above the deck, and the other to the forestay. They tie the port and starboard lines to the lifelines with clove hitches with a running bight, and can use them to adjust the scoop to compensate for any wind-against-tide angle the boat assumes. The scoop can be used in light wind. If a shower occurs, they untie the upper lines and drop the scoop down the forehatch.

These canvas squares have many other uses on board. For example, they can cover small on-deck paint or glue jobs in case of showers, act as cushion protectors during engine work, or be used as a collision mat to help stop water from flooding in if the hull is fractured.

Dodger guard

Canvas cockpit dodgers are vulnerable to falling booms and falling people; they also can make climbing into and out of the cockpit difficult, as they don't offer any firm hand-holds to hurrying crew. Allan Wallis, a New Zealand offshore sailor, solved both problems with a dodger guard.

The fabricated stainless-steel guard offers a firm hand grip and can also be used as a rack for solar panels. It's firmly attached to the cabintop with backing plates beneath each of its four feet. A piece of wood could be bolted to the upper rail of the guard and notched to work as a boom gallows.

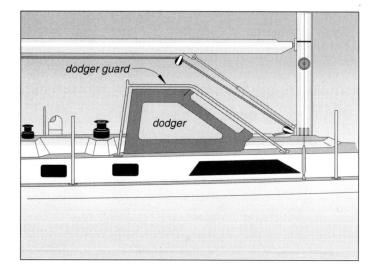

Painting/ Adhesives

Bottom painting

From Australian Uwe Laab comes a variation on the idea of painting the bottom with a different-color first coat so you can tell when it's time to repaint. He uses three coats of a hard anti-fouling paint first, on top of which he puts five coats of a different-color self-polishing or ablative paint. Although this is considerably more expensive than a conventional paint job, he claims it gave his boat a clean and growth-free bottom during a full two years in the tropics. Check with the manufacturer to ensure the two paints you use are compatible.

Propeller fouling

Should you use anti-fouling paint on your propeller? And even if you do, how long does it last? Uwe Laab suggests regularly coating the prop with water-pump grease, which can be applied under water. He claims it worked well for him in the tropics. We have never tried this, but we have spent an hour or so on several occasions scraping heavy growth off the prop. Even when clean, the surface remains rough with barnacle residue. A polished, greased prop would be a definite improvement.

Seized seizing

A quickie comes from Mark Humphries and Susie Anderson, who sail *Sweet Dreams,* a 30-foot Irwin, out of Galveston, Texas. They write, "The braided nylon used to secure the baby netting on our boat's lifelines tended to untie too easily. We found that a drop of Super Glue neatly locks such knots forever." Since discovering this, they have used Super Glue on everything from the sewn ends on whippings to the leather knots on their boat shoes. An industrial-size bottle is now part of their onboard fix-it kit.

Mixing small quantities of epoxy

Fritz Wood, who skippers his ketch, *Gaviota,* out of Road Town, Tortola, BVI, has come up with one of those simple ideas that make us wonder why we never thought of it. When measuring out tiny amounts of epoxy for a small repair job, he cuts two strips of 1-inch-by-6-inch rigid cardboard, uses one for each epoxy component, and then mixes the two parts together. A related suggestion from *Red Shoes* is the use of tongue depressors for the same purpose. A bunch of either is worth its weight in wood.

Varnish-removal aid

John Hazen, Jr. of Windward Pilgrim, Kaneohe Bay, Hawaii, writes, "I am removing a lot of old varnish from the 10-year-old, badly maintained Flicka I just purchased. I used to be a cabinetmaker and learned to use and appreciate cabinet scrapers. I have been using a cheap and disposable substitute scraper that I buy at the local building-materials outlet. Look for these substitutes in bins labeled 'joist hangers,' 'post-anchors,' 'beam ties,' and the like; I pay about 25 cents for them.

"Simpson Strong Ties are pieces of galvanized sheet metal that are stamped out on a machine. They are drilled and bent into various shapes for connecting framing members in house building. My favorite is a nailing plate, a rectangle about 2 inches by 5 inches, which has several rows of tiny holes drilled through it. The holes aren't important, but the burr that is created when this nailing plate is stamped out is. I choose the ones that have the most pronounced burr around all four edges. I use paint remover, wait 15 minutes, and then go to work with my 25-cent scrapers, throwing them away when they are dull."

The various other Simpson Strong Ties could be useful for getting at old varnish in difficult corners. These scrapers can be sharpened by running a fine file across the burr.

Drip-proof varnish pot

When you are varnishing or painting, an overloaded brush makes for less-than-perfect finishes. Wiping the brush on the side of the can not only introduces bubbles into the finish, but eventually makes for a messy, sticky can and an overloaded, bubble-laden brush. Wes Golemon of Oxnard, California, describes his perfect varnish can, one with a cut wire for brush wiping, that solves this problem. He uses a small, flat can and strings a piece of bailing wire tightly between two holes that he has punched out of either side of the can. The holes are positioned about ¼ inch below the rim and are offset from an imaginary centerline so that the wire will not interfere with dipping the brush. When he is finished varnishing, he rinses the pot just once with thinner and stores it upside-down. It stays clean and will last for years because the residual coating of varnish that is left behind seals the can against rust.

Varnish touch-up

Pat Mora, aboard *Alla Blanca*, cleaned an empty nail-polish bottle with acetone and filled it with his favorite varnish. A nail-polish bottle, if you haven't noticed, has a brush attached to the cap. Touching up is now easy—no getting out the badger hair from under glass, no painstaking cleanup with mineral spirits—and because it's so convenient, the job gets done.

Freezer brush and paint storage

An effective bristle-brush storage technique that we've used for years comes from Francis Mallory, who is presently restoring a vintage mahogany boat in Athens, Georgia. When you've finished painting or varnishing for the day, wrap your still-wet brush with plastic wrap and store it in the freezer. It will keep for a month or more and still be pliant and ready to go. Francis has tried this with oil-based paint, but it works equally well with water-based paint. A related tip: If you've mixed too much two-part paint, you can put it in the freezer and it'll keep for, well, significantly longer than if you didn't. Your ice cubes may taste like a boatyard, but given the cost of paint these days…

Rigging
Line hangers

Joseph O'Flynn of Summers Point, New Jersey, makes line hangers out of self-stick Velcro. He cuts 1 foot strips, removes the backing, and sticks the two lengths together, back to back. He loops the Velcro around coiled line and a stanchion, the Velcro sticks to itself, and the line is hung.

Rings instead of pins

Nick Reynolds of Vancouver, Washington, uses clevis rings instead of cotter pins on his boat's turnbuckles. Reynolds writes: "These are the little stainless-steel wire rings that hold clevis pins in place. Installation takes two twisting efforts for each clevis ring. First I twist the ring on the body of the turnbuckle (open-bodied turnbuckles only, of course), and then I repeat the process to get the ring in the hole in the end of the turnbuckle's threaded portion. When I remove the ring for adjustment, I can't lose it because it's still around the body of the turnbuckle. The change meets all my objectives: It holds the turnbuckle, it doesn't tear the sail, it looks good, and it's really cheap."

Line cutter/soldering gun

Having lived aboard our Crealock 34 for seven years, Nancy and I can tell you in two words why the average cruising boat is now 40 feet plus: Storage space. Thus, we love tools that can do double duty, such as a battery-powered drill that's also a screwdriver or, as with this submission, a soldering gun with an extra tip that's modified to cut line.

This idea comes from Jim Miller of Simsbury, Connecticut, who sails an Aqua Cat. Jim took a hammer to the business end of the soldering gun and flattened it to the thickness of a credit card. He recommends using a number of light blows rather than pounding rapidly, which could crack the tip. Then file any rough edges. Remember to carry a soldering gun that doesn't draw too many amps for your boat's inverter.

Rope-work tool

For marlinspike work, R.F. Hunt of Annapolis, Maryland, uses an electric butane stove lighter to melt the ends of synthetic lines, which prevents them from fraying.

Heat the bitter end of the line until soft. Work the hot end of the line against a metal surface to form the end of the line to any shape you want. It's easy to make pointed ends on small-diameter lines to form Turk's heads and the like, or to make rounded ends on halyards and sheets.

Clean-cut lines

Michael Bishop from Boulder, Colorado, who sails *Princess Elena,* a Beneteau First 285, heats an old hacksaw blade with a propane torch or stove to make a clean cut in synthetic lines. For the cleanest cut, he recommends cutting three-quarters of the way through, rotating the line, and finishing the cut from the other side.

Whipping with floss

Writing from Laurel, Delaware, Matt Blaine says he found himself with lines to whip but no waxed twine in his sail locker. Inspiration sent him to the medicine cabinet in search of dental floss. "It worked great," he says, "and comes waxed or unwaxed in a nifty dispenser that stows well and has a built-in cutter." Blaine claims that plain dental floss has worked well aboard his sailboat, *Harmony.* "If you want to get exotic, you can get mint flavored. This gives the imaginative sailor the option of not only color-coding his lines, but flavor-coding them." Sounds like a tasty idea.

A modern monkey fist

From Tony Hunter of Corpus Christi, Texas, comes an idea for a convenient heaving line. He writes, "For the past couple of years I have been using a softball to replace the sailor's traditional monkey fist. Because the softball has a cork interior, it floats and does not become waterlogged. I used an awl, marine twine, and a sail needle to stitch a piece of leather to the ball cover; it forms a strap long enough that a piece of ¼-inch line can be secured to the ball. I form this line into a small loop." Then Tony uses a bowline to secure a slightly larger (⅜-inch-diameter) heaving line to the monkey fist. His estimate of three times the length of the boat as an adequate heaving line seems about right. He recommends tying a large loop so the line can be dropped over a convenient bollard.

Tony continues, "For throwing, hold three loose coils of the heaving line plus the softball in your throwing hand; coil the rest of the line loosely and hold it in the other hand. Throw the softball underhanded to carry the line toward shore. Since most people are familiar with a softball, they will not be intimidated by seeing one flying in their direction. This should help them to catch it and the line. If the heaving line is to be thrown on board another boat, there is little chance of the softball doing any damage to that boat or to its crew."

Long-time passagemakers Lin and Larry Pardey, too, have used a heaving line to help other people guide their boat into a Mediterranean mooring situation and agree with Tony that one should be kept handy in a cockpit locker. Theirs is stored with the line coiled inside a canvas bag and the monkey fist outside, ready to grab in a hurry.

Easier masthead work

When Carlton Wilks worked at the masthead of *Sandra,* his Hunter 34, he found the bosun's chair didn't take him all the way to the top. To make his high life easier, he installed two folding steps (purchased from a marine supply store) about 5 feet from the masthead. After ascending as far as possible in the chair, he puts his feet on the steps, attaches a safety strap, and works like a lineman on a telephone pole. Says Carlton, "The steps are high enough to make a comfortable work platform. I can see what I'm doing, and my arms and hands are above the masthead." He advises keeping the bosun's chair strapped to you at all times in the unlikely event that both the steps and the safety strap fail.

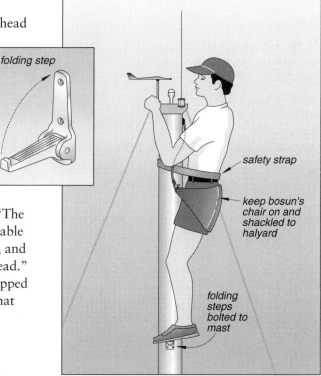

folding step

safety strap

keep bosun's chair on and shackled to halyard

folding steps bolted to mast

A more comfortable bosun's chair

An idea that I'm adopting aboard *Red Shoes* comes from Gary Paulin, who sails a San Juan 30 out of Mercer Island, Washington. Anyone who's spent time aloft knows how uncomfortable a bosun's chair can be. Gary made his chair more comfortable by adding stirrups. He took two 6-foot lengths of 1-inch nylon webbing and tied a loop in each end for his feet. When aloft, he tied the free end of each webbing strap to the lifting rings on his bosun's chair at a comfortable length. He's more comfortable in the chair now, even after several hours. He's since improved his invention by threading short lengths of flexible plastic tubing over the webbing at the stirrups to hold the loops open for his feet. The stirrups not only support the weight of his legs, but also allow him to shift his weight in the seat. The webbing is available at marine stores or rock-climbing suppliers. Gary says that at less than $2 to make, the stirrups are a lot cheaper than going to a chiropractor.

Gybe, no!

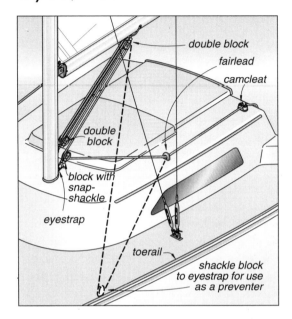

Harvey Wilson rigged a preventer for his Morgan 22, *Mity Mite*, which he sails on Stockton Lake, Missouri. He uses two double nonswivel blocks, ⅜-inch line, and a separate (larger) single swivel block with a fixed-bail snapshackle. The standing part leads to a camcleat on the cabintop (see illustration). When sailing downwind, he moves the single block from the base of the mast to an eyestrap on the toerail. This maintains vang control of the boom, with no worries about an accidental gybe.

Topping-lift control

Michael Koppstein of Ogunquit, Maine, developed an innovative mainboom topping-lift control. Traditionally, the topping lift either is left to flog around while the mainsail is hoisted or connected to a long length of shockcord run from the deck up the backstay to a swivel, whipped onto the backstay, and then redirected and attached via a thimble to the topping lift. This system requires constant adjustments according to point of sail and has limited life and looks.

Koppstein's innovation involves two small blocks, one with a sheave that fits the topping-lift wire and one that fits the backstay wire. To set up your own control, start by disassembling each block and reassembling each one around the cable that it fits.

While your boat is tied up at a dock, lift the boom to the height it achieves with the mainsail raised. Send a crewmember up the backstay in a bosun's chair to approximately the height of the first spreader (or halfway up the mainsail luff). Tighten the topping lift and measure the distance between it and the backstay. Cut a piece of shockcord 6 inches shorter than this distance and whip each end to one of the blocks.

Now the blocks will run up and down the backstay with changes in the tension on the shockcord. The "bungy block" system keeps the topping lift from chafing and disturbing wind release on the mainsail leech.

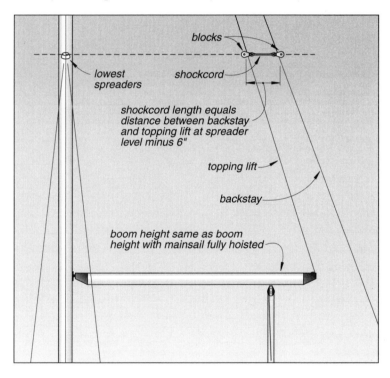

blocks

lowest spreaders

shockcord

shockcord length equals distance between backstay and topping lift at spreader level minus 6"

topping lift

backstay

boom height same as boom height with mainsail fully hoisted

No more flopping topping lifts

Jeff Hooper, writing from Newport Beach, California, has skippered cruising boats of all sizes and claims this idea worked even on the 100-foot *Whale's Tale*. To keep the topping lift from flopping around, first attach one end of a 6-foot length of the heaviest shockcord available to the end of the boom. Support the boom at a right angle to the mast, and loosen the topping lift. Stretch the shockcord to the maximum length along the topping lift, leaving enough slack to re-attach the end to the boom, and mark the topping lift at the end of the shockcord. Then release the shockcord from the boom, and attach it to the topping lift at the mark. Jeff has used various methods to secure the shockcord to the topping lift; he says seizing is the most secure and permanent method, but another quick-and-dirty option is a hose clamp wrapped with tape. Stretch the shockcord, and secure it to the end of the boom.

According to Jeff, once you get the topping lift properly adjusted, which requires experimentation, you may never have to make topping-lift adjustments again. I suggest using a temporary means of fastening the shockcord to the topping lift until you're sure you have the tension right. Be sure to protect from chafing, as a flogging hose clamp that's not taped could destroy a leech in short order.

Topping-lift ring

Conrad and Charlotte Skladal of Sunnyvale, California, have completed a 10-year-plus circumnavigation on their cutter, *Wisp*. One modification they made as they sailed provides extra places to secure lines at deck level without using cleats. They write: "We have found two-inch-diameter stainless-steel rings (made of ⅛-inch tubing) to be very useful as an attachment point for the ends of halyards, as well as for keeping the main topping lift secure. We simply slipped the rings between our turnbuckle toggle and the turnbuckle on the lower shrouds.

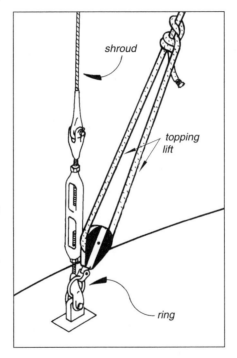

"To make an adjustable topping lift, we shackled a single block to the ring and led the bitter end of the topping lift through the block and up to where we secured it back on itself with a rolling hitch. We can adjust the height of the end of the main-boom by sliding the rolling hitch up and down the standing line. There's no need for a cleat, and the deck is clear of lines."

Storing a removable staysail stay

Joseph Colletto, of Tiburon, California, provides shippy storage of an idle staysail stay on his Rafiki 37 by running the stay around a grooved teak block and back to a padeye on deck. The interesting twist is his use of copper bolts, which are normally used in electrical work to join copper cables. The bolts have a slot that fits over both the forward lower shroud and the idle stay, securing them (finger-tight only) so the staysail stay won't flog the shroud. We've seen a similar set-up that used a snatch block instead of a grooved teak block.

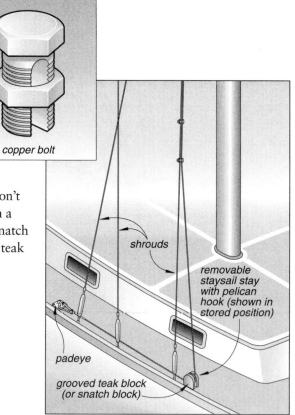

copper bolt

shrouds

removable staysail stay with pelican hook (shown in stored position)

padeye

grooved teak block (or snatch block)

Make your own spreader boots

If you're far away from a spreader-boot store, this idea might come in handy. Take a piece of clear- or white-plastic hose and cut as shown; fold each piece around the spreader tips, and tape the upper and lower ends around the shroud. Virginia Schultz of Kent, Ohio, made this idea work when her marine store was out of the proper-size boots for *Beau Geste,* her Bristol 24.

trim corners of hose as shown

slit hose

8"–12"

³/₄" or 1" plastic hose

spreader

tape tubing to shroud

shroud

Do-it-yourself shroud covers

To me, this solution, contributed by Floridian Edward Manzer, gives better results than using the stuff you can buy that fits the shroud snugly (and incidentally doesn't go over the turnbuckle.) Manzer buys 10-foot lengths of light PVC pipe and cuts them in half. He then disconnects the turnbuckle from the chainplate and slides the PVC up the shroud. Once the shroud is reattached and tuned, the pipe is allowed to drop down to cover the turnbuckle.

To find the proper-diameter PVC pipe, Manzer took short (less than 1 inch) samples, cut them lengthwise, and slipped them over the shroud (the samples will open enough to squeeze over the wire). Another advantage: Because stainless steel corrodes slower if it's not confined (as it is when taped), using PVC pipe allows it to breathe. It's also easy to slide the PVC upward for eyeball inspection of the swage, StaLok, or another fitting. I do wonder about the rattling in a blow, however.

No more cleat hangups

Most sailors have had a sheet or line catch on a foredeck cleat when gybing or tacking, and it's no fun to scurry forward to dislodge it. This remedy comes from Robert Johnson, who sails *Windfinder II,* a Tanzer 22. Robert routed out a two-by-four and beveled the outside until it fit over the troublesome cleat on his foredeck. He uses shockcord to hold the two-by-four in place. Now wayward lines won't catch on the smooth surface, and the block can be easily removed when the cleat is needed. On *Red Shoes* such an item could have saved many a blue exclamation!

Reefing aid for roller-reefing jibs

Ron Beck sends this great idea from *Wendy Sails,* a Cal 39 in Orlando, Florida. Some-

cleat, but it will be easy to release. Fiddle blocks aren't cheap, but in severe weather this idea could make a difficult job possible and thus be worth the money.

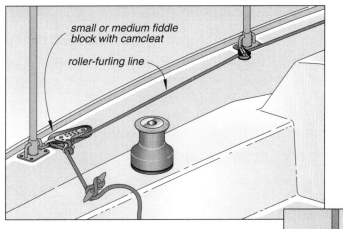

small or medium fiddle block with camcleat

roller-furling line

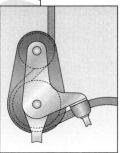

times when it's blowing hard and you want to reef the jib, you have to use a winch. Then, once you've reefed it, you need to free the winch for other purposes—unless you have a dedicated winch or rope clutch. During the transfer from the winch to a cleat, the flogging jib starts to unroll. To hold the furling line while making the transfer, Beck runs it through a fiddle block with a camcleat. If you don't have an aluminum toerail with lots of holes, you'll probably need to install a padeye for the fiddle block. If rigged as shown in the drawing, the camcleat will hold the furling line while you make the line fast to another

Halyard wrap on a roller-furler?

James Chowning and his wife, Joan, used to sail their Pearson Wanderer, *Notre Amour,* on Chesapeake Bay. James came up with a way to prevent a roller-furling jib halyard from wrapping. We haven't tried this yet, but we plan to. If the luff of your roller-furling jib doesn't extend all the way to the sheave on the mast, consider threading the exposed halyard through a length of PVC pipe equal to the distance from the luff to the mast sheave. This arrangement should prevent the halyard from wrapping around the furled jib. Be sure to file any rough edges on the pipe to minimize chafe.

No more halyard wrap

Everyone with headsail roller-furling must beware of halyard wrap, as the exposed halyard(s) at the top of the forestay can wrap around the headstay and jam the gear. Joseph Colletto of Tiburon, California, has used to great advantage an idea found in many sailboat manuals: Adding a bracket-mounted sheave to the front of the mast (see illustration). Although this adds halyard friction because it increases the angle of the halyard where it attaches to the furling unit, it also makes halyard wrap virtually impossible.

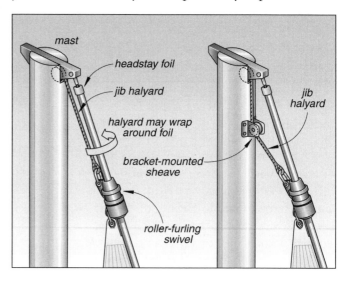

Inexpensive shroud cleats

Joseph Young of Newton, Massachusetts, sails a Stone Horse and claims that the shroud cleats he makes are cheaper and less likely to snag lines than commercial shroud cleats (see illustration). He uses a stainless-steel U-bolt and a nickel-size slug for a backing plate. He drills two holes in the slug to accept the U-bolt and then inserts a stainless-steel ring in the curved part of the U-bolt, which is attached to the shroud. He assembles the pieces and tightens the nuts, being careful not to crush the shroud wires. It's important to attach the cleats to the lower shrouds, as putting them on the uppers may result in jibsheet snags.

Midship cleat

Virginians Lance and Karen Pearson have a good suggestion for boats with aluminum toerails. Wanting a midship cleat for spring lines, they fastened a teak block with a horn cleat to the inside of the rail with screws (bolts with recessed nuts might be stronger). *Dulcimer,* their Irwin 34, can now accommodate spring lines without using the chafe-making holes in the aluminum rail.

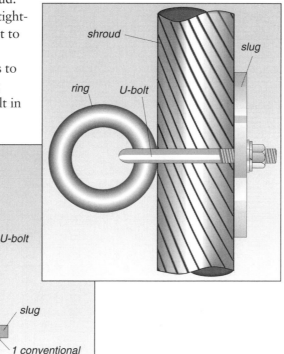

Cutting rigging wire

Richard Weinberg, who sails *Le Grand Bleu*, a Hunter 26.5, out of Casco Bay, Maine, has come up with this idea to cut rigging wire cleanly without cable cutters. All you need, he says, is a scrap two-by-four, a drill, and a hacksaw with a sharp, fine-tooth blade. Drill a hole the exact diameter of the wire you're cutting near one corner of the wide side of the two-by-four (see illustration). Then cut a groove perpendicular to the hole through the short side of the two-by-four with the hacksaw, making sure that the groove bisects the hole completely. Mark the wire, and slide the free end through the hole. Sight through the groove until the spot you've marked on the wire is lined up with the groove. Hold the wire in place by clamping it with Vise-Grips on either side of the board, and saw through the groove. This keeps the end of the wire from coming unlaid, and the cut will be clean and square.

Cutting wire rope

There are two conventional ways to cut wire rope on a boat: using a hacksaw and using boltcutters. The object is to keep the wires from becoming unlaid during the cut. Tape can help, but one reader may have come up with a better solution. Hugh Poling of Carnation, Washington, sails *Tough Puff,* a Cal 21, and says that the small cutoff disks used with a Dremel grinder work well and cut cleanly through wire rope. Hugh was using a battery-powered Dremel for another job and realized that since it wasn't tied to 110-volt shore power, it made a fine tool to cut wire rope on a boat.

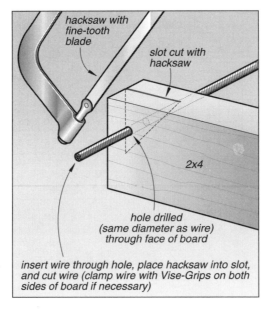

hacksaw with fine-tooth blade

slot cut with hacksaw

2x4

hole drilled (same diameter as wire) through face of board

insert wire through hole, place hacksaw into slot, and cut wire (clamp wire with Vise-Grips on both sides of board if necessary)

Sails

Tie-downs for mainsails

Cam von Wahlde of Park Ridge, Illinois, controls the flaked mainsail on his O'Day sloop with a method that doesn't require screw holes in the boom or mast. He started with a doubled length of shockcord about a foot longer than his boom. He then threaded four nylon hooks onto the shockcord and knotted the double length together in four places (with a hook between each pair of knots). He secured the shockcord to each end of the boom with an existing padeye near the mast and a tang at the outer end of the boom.

When the sail is lowered and flaked, he pulls the hooks over the sail and clips them to the length of parallel shockcord. The result is a zig-zag pattern along the boom that keeps the sail in place. The distance between knots can be varied to regulate tension and keep the sail tightly flaked. For smaller boats ⅛-inch shockcord works well, but use a larger diameter for big boats.

This strikes me as an excellent system, and I intend to adopt it for *Red Shoes*. However, instead of knotting the parallel lines of shockcord, I'll tie bits of line over the shockcord using a rolling hitch at the points where I think the knots should be. These can easily be loosened and adjusted.

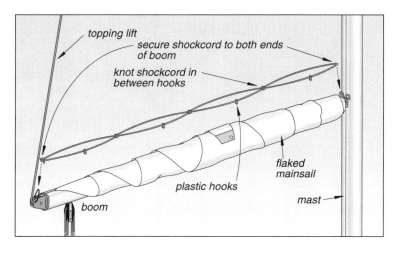

topping lift

secure shockcord to both ends of boom

knot shockcord in between hooks

flaked mainsail

plastic hooks

mast

boom

Roller-furling headsail security

Here's a good idea from Bud Greene of Lake Worth, Florida. When he secures his Hunter 36, *Wild Goose,* in its slip, he makes sure the roller-furling jib stays put by wrapping a spare jib halyard around the furled sail (using a downward spiral) and attaching the shackle to the bow pulpit. "The procedure takes only five minutes, and the added security has helped my peace of mind many times in a blow."

Genoa-track alternative

When Willard Boyle from Wallace, Nova Scotia, tried to install a genoa track on his Seadrift pocket cruiser, he found there was no space to install it. "The boat came equipped with jib-furling gear, but there was no way to effectively adjust the lead on the jibsheet," he says. "The deficiency was particularly notice-able when sailing to windward with the jib partially furled." Forced to improvise, he installed a turning block on the cabintop and ran a line through the block to a free-running block on the jibsheet. The jib can now be closehauled by shortening the auxiliary line to the free-running block. The resulting arrange-ment allows Boyle to adjust sail shape and keep the jibsheet under control when tacking.

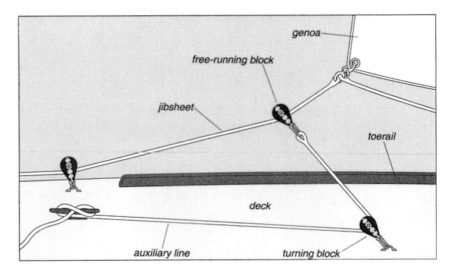

Jib net

A jib net can keep sails or other gear through your foredeck lifelines. Here's an idea from Skip Allan of Capitola, California, who fitted a simple and attractive one to his boat with minimal cost and labor. He used parachute cord and small padeyes. The padeyes were fixed to the deck at 12-inch centers, from the bow pulpit to the shrouds, as closely as possible to directly below the lifelines. The parachute cord was laced along from the bottom lifeline from the pulpit to the shrouds by alternately passing the line through the padeyes and over the lifeline. Skip then took another line, secured it at the pulpit, and laced it from the upper lifeline through the lower lacing and back to the upper lifeline. He tied off the end of the upper line with a rolling hitch to keep it from sliding.

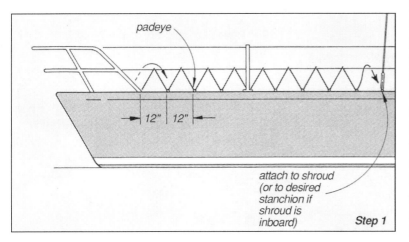

padeye

12" 12"

attach to shroud (or to desired stanchion if shroud is inboard)

Step 1

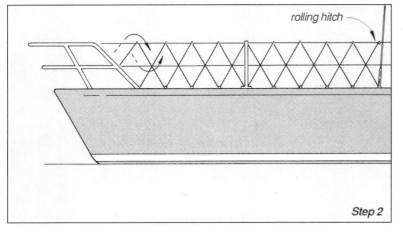

rolling hitch

Step 2

Ripstop nylon-drifter repair

Laura Posamentier sent us this repair method that she used for the nylon drifter on *Sola,* her Pacific Seacraft 25. She bought waterproof fabric glue (Aleene's "OK to Wash-It") at a craft shop for $3.79. It applies just like Elmer's glue, but it's waterproof after a 24-hour cure. At a local fabric store she bought a ripstop nylon swatch that matched the color of her drifter. She cut a patch that overlapped the rip in the drifter by at least 1 inch all around, spread the glue evenly around the area, and installed the patch.

After the 24-hour curing period, she sewed on the patch with a zig-zag stitch. A regular Singer sewing machine with a ballpoint needle handles the job nicely. She tells us that this glue not only forms a strong bond, but it also prevents further fraying of the fabric. "The hardest part of the job was finding a large enough space to stretch out the sail." Laura sails out of Houston, Texas.

Canvas closure

Mary Richards, who is enjoying a cruising retirement on various sailboats, came up with an idea to secure a canvas mainsail cover on the underside of the boom (it works for other canvas covers, too). Mary doubles a short length of line and sews it together, leaving an eye at the loop end. She sews the middle of this "tadpole" to one edge of the canvas cover. To secure the cover around the flaked mainsail, she pushes the eye of the tadpole through a grommet on the other edge of the canvas and threads the tail through the eye.

As Nancy and I are about to make a new mainsail cover for *Red Shoes,* this idea struck a chord. Simple and inexpensive, it seems like a salty project with satisfying results.

No more rusty sewing needles

On *Red Shoes,* no matter where we keep our sail needles, they always rust. D.J. Brooks, an Ontarian who sails *The Nancy 0,* a CS30 sloop, has a good solution to the rusty-needle problem. He cuts a strip of flannel (longer than the largest needle) and soaks it with light oil. Then he weaves the needles into the cloth, rolls it up, and puts the oily bundle into a container. An empty plastic spice container works well, according to D.J., but you may have to eat a lot of garlic salt to get one.

Easier reefing

In strong winds, it's often difficult to twist the mainsail when trying to slip the reefing cringle onto the reefing hook. Mort Geller of New Bern, North Carolina, uses a good system on his Catalina 22, *Happy Hour*. He says, "Sew a D-ring onto one end of a short length of strong tubular webbing, such as sail-tie material. Thread the webbing through the reefing cringle, and sew another D-ring on the other end." When it's time to reef, just slip either D-ring onto the reefing hook, and the other D-ring will keep the webbing from pulling through the cringle. "This is a straight pull," he says, "and it eliminates the need to twist the sail in high winds." Remember to use strong webbing and D-rings that are too large to pass through the reefing cringle.

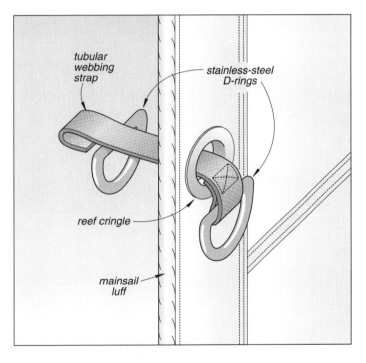

tubular webbing strap

stainless-steel D-rings

reef cringle

mainsail luff

Reefing convenience

Steve Christensen of Bay City, Michigan, found a way to expedite reefing aboard his Precision 23, *Kittiwake*. The reefing process had required removing a sail stop from the sail-slide groove so that the new tack cringle could be pulled down enough to reach the reefing hook. Not only was the stop difficult to remove at times, but if it wasn't replaced, the mainsail spilled out all over the deck when the halyard was eased. He set out to find a better way to reef.

He writes, "I needed a couple of narrow strips to screw over the opening in the sail track after the sail-track slides were inserted that would close off the track so that a sail stop would no longer be necessary. I went to my local ACE Hardware store and found just what I needed: ¾-inch-wide aluminum tile edging, sold in a 36-inch strip for only $2.75. The lip

on this edging is about the same thickness as that of the mast track itself, so the mainsail slides don't get hung up as they pass over the strips when the mainsail is raised or lowered.

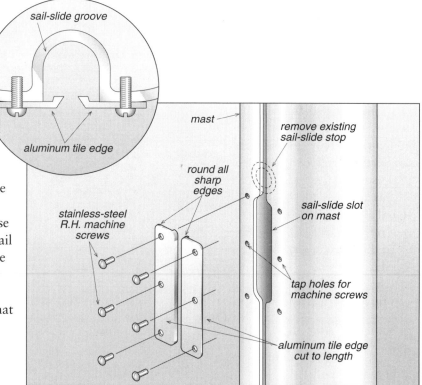

sail-slide groove

aluminum tile edge

mast

remove existing sail-slide stop

round all sharp edges

stainless-steel R.H. machine screws

sail-slide slot on mast

tap holes for machine screws

aluminum tile edge cut to length

S'nuff said

Have you ever had the sail fabric bunch up around the hoop of your snuffer as you try to douse your spinnaker? Steve Judson of Gambrills, Maryland, worked out this solution aboard *Fireworks,* his Ranger 23. Figuring a sort of funnel would help feed the material through the hoop, he modified a plastic washbasin and attached it to the bottom of the sock at the hoop. The basin had a bottom diameter slightly larger than the hoop's. He cut a hole with the same diameter as the inner diameter of the hoop in the bottom of the basin. Holes drilled around the circumference allowed it to be lashed to the hoop with small-diameter line, and he used a soldering iron to melt corresponding holes in the sock. "Finally," Steve writes, "I pulled the sock through the large hole in the bottom of the basin so the basin was upside down. The hoop rested against the inside of the basin and was lashed in place. I reattached the sock halyard and downhaul bridles, attached to the hoop, around the hoop and edge of the hole in the bottom of the basin. I found it helpful to run the downhaul bridle outside the basin and attach it on each side of the basin rim."

Easy spinnaker handling

Julie Palm, aboard the Tayana *52 Sojourner,* offers a solution for shorthanded spinnaker handling. She finds that a spinnaker trip line allows the crew to take down the chute with as few as two people—one in the cockpit and one on the foredeck. As a result, flying the spinnaker has become *Sojourner*'s normal downwind sailplan.

"We use a light ¼-inch trip line about 15 feet long. When setting up our spinnaker pole, the foredeck person threads the trip line forward through the downhaul shackle on the bottom of the pole, through the release ring of the guy shackle, and back through a padeye on top of the pole. A figure eight or other stopper knot is tied at the forward end of the line. The other end is tied to a lifeline with enough slack so the pole can move freely without tripping the guy.

"When it is time to lower the chute, the foredeck person pulls the trip line to release the guy and then pulls the takedown line for the spinnaker sock. No one has to stand precariously on the bow pulpit to 'stab' the guy shackle. We now feel safe and secure, knowing we can always release the guy from the chute quickly in a sudden gust."

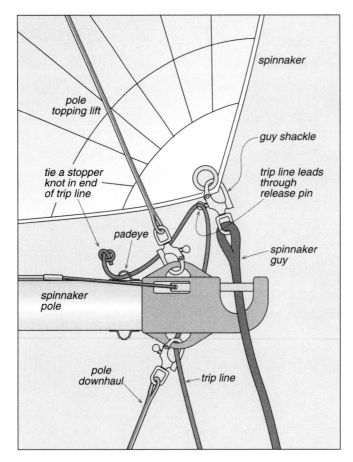

- spinnaker
- pole topping lift
- guy shackle
- tie a stopper knot in end of trip line
- trip line leads through release pin
- padeye
- spinnaker guy
- spinnaker pole
- pole downhaul
- trip line

Small-boat whisker pole

On a boat, and particularly on one the size of Doug Johnson's Holder 14, any multiple-use idea is like gold. Johnson, who lives in Andover, Kansas, has adapted his paddle for use as a whisker pole (see illustration). He cut the eye off a bronze snap and drilled a hole

snaphook (not shown), that's just large enough to receive a 4-penny galvanized nail for retention (a purist might want to try a bronze pin to avoid electrolysis). He then cut a slot in the end of the paddle just large enough for the jibsheet. My only question: Does the snaphook interfere with paddling? Perhaps it would be better if it were removable.

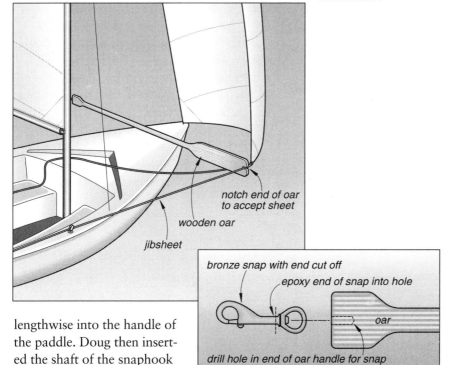

notch end of oar
to accept sheet

wooden oar

jibsheet

bronze snap with end cut off

epoxy end of snap into hole

oar

drill hole in end of oar handle for snap

lengthwise into the handle of the paddle. Doug then inserted the shaft of the snaphook into the hole, secured it with epoxy, and drilled a small hole, cross-wise through both the paddle and the shaft of the

Batten storage

Mike Kison of Pearland, Texas, uses a 48-inch length of 2-inch PVC pipe to store sail battens for his JY15. He sanded one end of the tube to make a PVC cap easier to take on and off and then permanently glued another PVC cap to the other end. For a nice touch Mike drilled a hole in the tube and the removable cap and strung a short lanyard between them so the cap wouldn't be lost. On *Red Shoes* we use a similar system (6-inch PVC pipe) to store charts. Although I'd rather store them flat, our chart library won't fit otherwise.

No more battens overboard

Tired of losing battens overboard, Patrice Baker of Clifton Park, New York, has discovered another use for Velcro. All too often a batten would manage to shake loose from its pocket, hit the water, and sink out of sight while Patrice was reefing, hoisting, or dropping the mainsail. After some research, she purchased a 2-inch-wide strip of Velcro to equal the width of the batten pocket, as well as some Velcro adhesive. She then sewed a 3-inch length of the loop side of the Velcro to the leech of the sail near the end of the batten pocket. Next she glued the hook side of the Velcro, hooks out, to the outside of the batten pocket. The 3-inch tape of Velcro folds over the pocket opening and locks the batten in place.

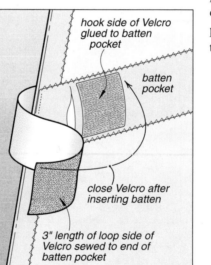

hook side of Velcro glued to batten pocket

batten pocket

close Velcro after inserting batten

3" length of loop side of Velcro sewed to end of batten pocket

Rigid sail bags

Martin Browne of Brookline, Massachusetts, has a simple way to carefully car-top resinated one-design sails. Browne states, "When my wife and I bought our Sonar (a 23-foot one-design racer/daysailer), we had a problem fitting the carefully rolled tubes of resinated

"Our sails can now be tied on top of the car without bending, creasing, or otherwise damaging the finish of the sails or the car."

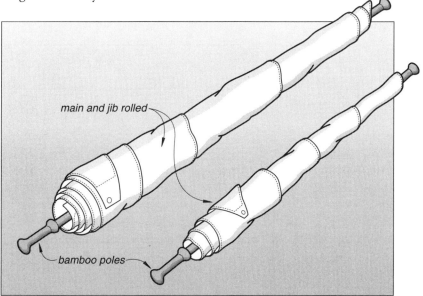

main and jib rolled

bamboo poles

sails onto our car without bending them." They bought some bamboo poles, cut them to the appropriate lengths for each rolled sail, and pushed them into the bagged sails for support. Bamboo is cheap, light, and easily cut using a normal wood saw. Martin says,

Sail folding made simple

Like many people who learn to sail at a school, Harvey Wallace of San Jose, California, was frustrated when the techniques he was taught didn't include ways to fold a jib on board so it would fit in the often undersized sail bags supplied by sailmakers. His solution for folding a headsail on the small foredeck of a 27-foot boat is worth sharing and can be done at anchor or at sea.

Wallace writes, "Use one sheet to pull the clew back, and fasten it to the mast. If the jib has a longer J measurement (the length of the jib's foot, or the length from the clew to the tack) than the length of the foredeck, you may have to stretch the foot past the mast and attach it temporarily at some other point. I hoist the jib loosely and leave a wrap of the halyard around the winch; then I ease the halyard slowly with one hand while I use my other hand to fold the sail back and forth as it falls onto the foredeck. If there's a breeze, I use one foot to hold the fold in place while I lower the sail to make the next fold. (Be careful not to put your weight on that foot, or you may slip.) Once the entire jib is down and folded from foot to head, I remove all the jib hanks and then fold it from tack to clew. With a little practice, I learned to determine how tightly I needed to fold the jib to get it to fit inside my bag."

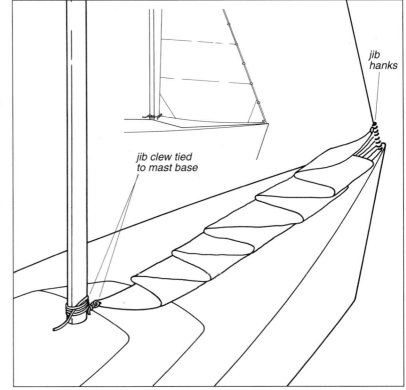

jib hanks

jib clew tied to mast base

Interior

Centerboard pusher

Centerboards have been known to become stuck in the raised position at the most inopportune times. All it takes is some sand or barnacles to jam the board inside the slot. Boat designer Roberto Hosmann of Buenos Aires, Argentina, has come up with an effective solution to the problem. His sketches detail a centerboard-pushing mechanism that can be retrofitted to many centerboard-trunk designs. Once installed, a threaded plug caps the tube and can be quickly replaced with a push rod when it's time to free a stuck centerboard. It takes just a few turns of the screw-driven rod to get rid of a problem that might otherwise spoil a cruise.

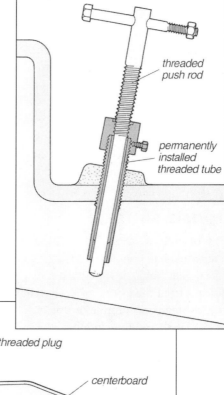

threaded push rod

permanently installed threaded tube

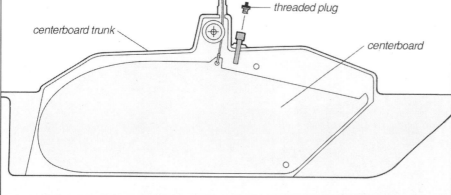

centerboard trunk

threaded plug

centerboard

Socket organizer

Dick Cartelli, who sails *Step Two,* a Venture 23, on Vermont's Lake Champlain, writes, "When the plastic organizing tray in my socket-set toolbox finally fell apart, I replaced it with my own. I uscd a small paintbrush to apply a thin coat of acetone to one socket and immediately placed it on a scrap piece of 14-inch Dow blueboard insulation. The acetone dissolved the blueboard and created a snug home for the handle and each socket. A thin coat of epoxy will keep the insulation from coming apart."

Small-parts storage

John Martin of Punta Gorda, Florida, uses clear-plastic tennis-ball containers for storage. Small parts such as bolts, hose clamps, and fuel-line fittings fit in the cylinders easily. The containers can organize a jumble of things, they're easy to label, and they won't rust. They sound ideal to me. How wonderful to look at a rustproof container and know instantly what's inside!

Locker locks

Seeking a positive closure for side-opening lockers in the galley of *Latigazo,* a Holman-designed 31-foot sloop, Gerald Stock bought brass window locks at Home Depot. "At about $7 apiece they weren't cheap, but they're secure and easy to open and close. They also look very nice," he says. Gerald notes that you may have to shim the clasp side of the lock during installation to ensure that the clasp will line up with its mate. He sails out of Jacksonville Beach, Florida.

Hatchboard stowage

Joe Hannabach was tired of scratching his varnished hatchboards, so he made a Sunbrella storage envelope that works much like an accordion file. "No need for padding or liners," says Hannabach. "Just cut out three pockets and a flap, and sew them together." Any reasonably rugged material will do, adds Hannabach, who sails *Lille Skat,* a Cal 28 sloop.

Hatchboard holder

Finding a place to put the hatchboards is one of sailing's greatest puzzles. Sandra Kelting Prendergast, aboard *Ka Sandera,* has an answer for boats with a two-board companionway that could be adapted for most boats with opening hatchboards.

She leaves the bottom hatchboard in place, as it is easy to step over and keeps items from falling through the companionway. Aft of this board, on the cockpit side of the companionway, she attached two small grooved strips identical to the track into which the hatchboards normally slide. The strips are through-bolted to the cabinhouse and hold the upper hatchboard securely against the lower hatchboard. Be sure to allow enough room for the hatchboards to swell when wet.

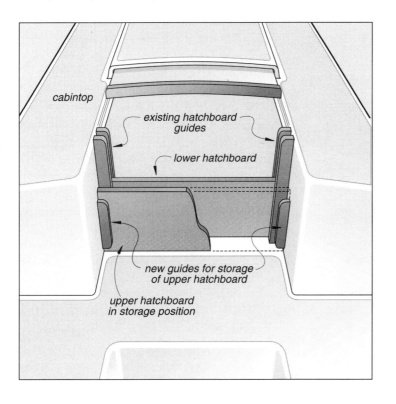

cabintop

existing hatchboard guides

lower hatchboard

new guides for storage of upper hatchboard

upper hatchboard in storage position

Removable anti-skid

On *Kiosk,* a Freedom 30, owner Robert Jenks places the anti-skid material often used under carpets on the cabin sole to prevent his cooler from sliding and making scratches while under sail. A similar rubbery, mesh-like material is sold in marine and hardware stores. It comes on a roll, and we use it on *Red Shoes* for keeping things from sliding on the sole, tables, and desktops.

Uncrazing hatches and ports

Plexiglas and Lexan tend to craze or cloud after years in the sun. Matt Delaney of Abington, Massachusetts, claims that while commercially available solutions work fairly well on a temporary basis, his method of rejuvenating old hatches lasts indefinitely with minimal care. He uses a wax compound block and a buffer with a wool pad. The block contains a hard wax and a substance called Tripoli, sometimes referred to as "jeweler's rouge." "One block," he says, "will probably last you the rest of your life if you use it only for the ports, but it also restores full finishes and makes boats look like new." When used on Plexiglas, the wax block removes the surface layer of material and seals the pores with a long-lasting wax. In extreme cases, the surface could be prepared prior to buffing by wet-sanding with 1,000-grit sandpaper on a sanding block. "Remember," Matt cautions, "buffer pads generate heat, so a light touch is more effective in the long run."

Keeping cushions in place

Aboard Don Ziliox's Rhodes 22, *Sneakie II,* the dinette becomes a berth, which is formed by piecing together several cushions. To prevent the cushions from shifting and exposing uncomfortable cracks during the night, Don put removable carpet anti-skid on the settees, and now the cushions stay in place. He also uses anti-skid on the cockpit seats to tame cushions when the boat heels.

More privacy

Stan Rempuszewski, who sails *Windwalker,* his Irwin 10/4, out of Kent Narrows in the Chesapeake, has found a simple and attractive privacy covering for opening portlights. He cut a piece of heavy paper to the exact size of the portlights for a template and traced this shape onto a vinyl placemat. He cut the placemat with scissors and fit the resulting cover against the screen, which is held in place by the closed portlight. If you don't have any screens, glue the cover to the glass itself with a thin layer of silicone seal at the corners or edge. Stan says, "With the wide array of placemat colors and styles available, it's easy to pick something that matches the boat's decor."

Convenient carry-all

Randall Harman, a full-time cruiser aboard *Oui Si,* a customized Yorktown 33, has learned the hard way that plastic garbage bags frequently tear before they reach the dumpster. To solve this problem, Harman made a strong, reusable storage bag from a plastic tarp material that's reinforced with fiberglass-thread mesh. The material can be cut with scissors and sewn with a regular sewing machine. After several wet dinghy trips from shore to anchorage, Harman discovered that another use for a bag of this type is to keep groceries and clean laundry protected from spray. A 6-foot-by-8-foot tarp works well and can be bought in most hardware stores for less than $4.

Water heater plus

Bernard Ahern often spends winter nights aboard his 1967 Texas Trimaran, *High Roller*. When the outside temperature dropped to below 50°F in his home port of Livonia, Louisiana, he found his unheated shower uncomfortably chilly. For the last three years he has used a 15-foot strip of drain-line heater to take the chill off the water in the tank. He taped the heater to one side of the 18-gallon water tank, holding it in place with aluminum tape. The heater requires 120-volt AC, but since it draws only 12 watts, even a light-duty inverter can easily power it. When used in a 12-volt system, the inverter will draw 1 amp.

An additional benefit to this system, says Bernard, is that the heater keeps the whole compartment dry. Other lengths and wattages of drain-line heater are available. He warns, however, to be sure not to overlap the heater strip during installation.

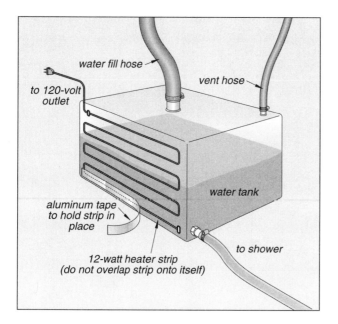

water fill hose

vent hose

to 120-volt outlet

water tank

aluminum tape to hold strip in place

to shower

12-watt heater strip (do not overlap strip onto itself)

City water pressure

"It's a pain to keep refilling my boat's water tanks all the time when I'm in a slip supplied with city water," writes Ralph Levitt. He connected the filler hose from the bib on the dock to his freshwater system to enjoy city water pressure without using his pressure pump or the water in his tanks.

To plumb his Island Packet 31, *Second Love,* for this, Levitt installed a Y-valve immediately after the boat's pressure-water pump. From there he ran a hose to a permanent fitting in the cockpit, to which the filler hose from the dock can be easily attached. He also attached a toggle shutoff valve to the filler hose, making it a simple (and dry) matter to disconnect the hose from the boat.

Levitt warns that city water pressure can be strong enough to burst hoses; he recommends that sailors adhere to ABYC (American Boat and Yacht Council) guidelines for plumbing. He installed a pressure reducer at the dock bib to protect the boat's plumbing from pressure-induced leaks, and he makes a point of turning off the dock faucet when he leaves the boat.

Flying-object holder

Bob and Ruth Palatnik of Tappan, New York, like the homey touch of decorative items on *Jade Queen,* their 47-foot Vagabond ketch, but not the hassle of stowing them every time they go sailing. So to make things stay put on either a vertical or horizontal surface, they apply a putty-like (and reusable) adhesive called Fun Tak. Fun Tak is a trademark of Dap, Inc. and is readily available in most supermarkets for under $2.

Simply tear off a chunk of adhesive of an appropriate size, roll it into a ball, work it until it is soft and tacky, and then slap it onto most any surface and attach the item to be secured.

Icebox drain

Icebox drains receive little consideration from most boatbuilders. Either the icebox drains into the bilge, or a complicated pump system drains the melted ice overboard. New Hampshire's John Torrison, who owns *Plover,* a Sabre 28, had an idea that's both simple and thoughtful. His icebox drained directly into the bilge and occasionally produced a foul odor that was hard to eliminate.

Inspiration hit when he surveyed his galley sink, which was plumbed with both a foot pump and a hand pump. He connected the spout to the foot pump, which draws water from the freshwater tank (see illustration). He then removed the hose that connected the icebox drain to the bilge and ran new hose from the icebox drain to the hand pump at the sink. "This arrangement," he tells us, "allows me to use the melted icewater for washing or rinsing dishes and stops any food spillage from entering the bilge. As an added bonus, it cuts the airflow within the icebox, so now the ice seems to last longer."

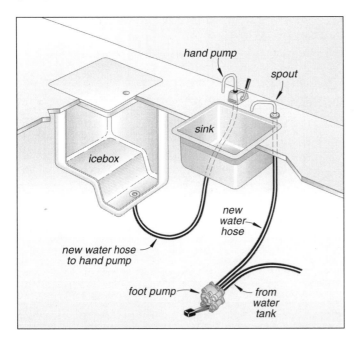

hand pump

spout

sink

icebox

new water hose

new water hose to hand pump

foot pump

from water tank

Combination pump

Galley sink awash? John Hollands, currently cruising Fijian waters, has a solution that serves two purposes: Using a manual pump and two-way valve to drain either your sink or bilge. He recommends connecting "a high-capacity manual bilgepump to the outlet side of a two-way selector valve, with the outlet side of the pump plumbed to the sink's through-hull seacock via a non-collapsible 1½-inch hose. The two inlet ports of the valve are then connected to the sink drain and the bilge. By selecting one or the other, you can use the pump to empty the sink and drain hose, eliminating the saltwater and odor problem; or you can use the same pump and through-hull to empty the bilge. You'll have to find room for the system under the sink. An access door to the sink drain and pump handle is a prerequisite. The fact that the sink drain must be kept closed after pumping to prevent salt water from backing up into the sink provides an extra measure of safety."

Add counter space

Jim Peters of Bethesda, Maryland, finds the galley workspace aboard his Catalina 27, *Windsong,* very limited. His solution is a sink-top cutting board that provides additional counter space for preparing food and remains secure even while under way.

Make or buy a cutting board that's large enough to cover the sink opening and just overlap the rim of the sink on all sides. Trim it to this size if necessary. On the underside of the cutting board, center another piece of wood that has been cut to fit the sink opening snugly, and secure the two together with stainless-steel wood screws.

Trailersailing
Anti-skid for an outboard fuel tank

When he tired of his steel outboard-fuel tank sliding to the other side of the well with every tack, John Iannacone of Tulsa, Oklahoma, came up with this idea. He cut a piece of $5/16$-inch rubber fuel-line hose to the same length as the circumference of the bottom of the fuel tank. He slit the hose lengthwise and fit it around the bottom lip of the tank. He claims no glue is needed. John sails *Ten Grand,* a Catalina 22, on Grand Lake.

Stop gas tanks from sliding

Bill Evans of Huntsville, Alabama, uses a rubber shower mat with suction cups to keep the metal outboard gasoline tank on his Catalina 25 from sliding back and forth when it's stored in its nook under the helmsperson's seat.

Outboard starter

Anyone who has used an adjustable outboard bracket on a trailerable boat knows that wrestling with a motor attached to one is awkward, uncomfortable, difficult, maddening, and dangerous in extreme conditions. Robert Bird of Miami, Florida, put a neat idea into use on his 24-foot sloop. He installed a starting rope that is 5 feet longer than stock, tied a stopper knot where the handle used to be, and installed the handle at the end of the line. This lets him crank the motor from a standing position in the cockpit rather than trying to do it while on his knees leaning over the transom. This idea may not put chiropractors out of business, but it could make life easier for trailersailors using an outboard for auxiliary power.

Outboard tilting made easier

The difficult task of tilting an outboard that's mounted low on the transom of your sailboat is made easier by this idea from Reinhold Klein, who lives in Bradenton, Florida, and sails *Winsome II,* a Precision 23. The illustration tells all, but basically it's a handy billy with a camcleat on the stern pulpit.

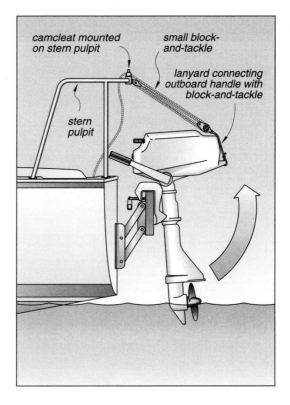

Quick shifter

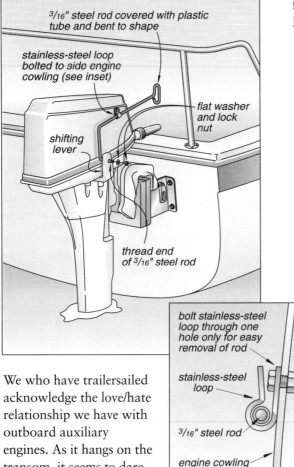

3/16" steel rod covered with plastic tube and bent to shape

stainless-steel loop bolted to side engine cowling (see inset)

flat washer and lock nut

shifting lever

thread end of 3/16" steel rod

bolt stainless-steel loop through one hole only for easy removal of rod

stainless-steel loop

3/16" steel rod

engine cowling

accompanying illustration. It's simple, easy to make, and effective. Thanks to Mike Booze from Loveland, Ohio, who sails *Nepenthe*, a MacGregor 25.

We who have trailersailed acknowledge the love/hate relationship we have with outboard auxiliary engines. As it hangs on the transom, it seems to dare you to stay cool and in command. One more weapon for skippers is the gear-shift control rod shown in the

Cure that broken step

A classy idea for a small boat comes from Bill Glover of Renton, Washington. On small racer/cruiser designs, a cooler is often incorporated as a companionway step, but the top won't stand up to long-term abuse. He solved this problem on *Paradigm Shift*, his Merit 25, by making a teak step and securing it to the top of the cooler with Velcro. The step can be easily removed when you take the cooler off the boat. Best of all, he says, there are no more broken tops.

Cockpit-sole grate as berth

This idea might be a boon to boats with a long cockpit and no intervening binnacle. Hamish Tear of Vail, Colorado, made a wood grate to line the cockpit sole of *About Ready*, his Catalina 22 (see illustration), that doubles as a handy cockpit berth for outside sleeping. He attached redwood strips to the sides of the

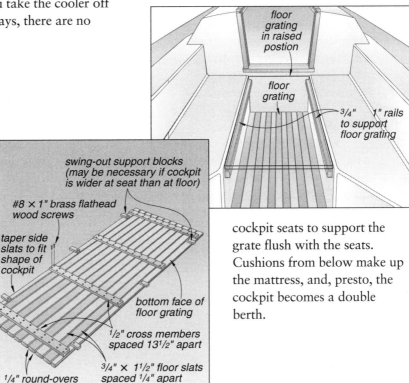

cockpit seats to support the grate flush with the seats. Cushions from below make up the mattress, and, presto, the cockpit becomes a double berth.

Trailering security for rigging

From Ray Newman, who trails and sails his Sea Fare 26, *Adeal,* on the Great Lakes, comes a way to secure stays and shrouds to the mast while trailering. He found that duct tape was effective but difficult to remove. As an alternative, Ray folds plastic trash bags the long way into 4-inch strips. He then wraps the bags around the mast and shrouds twice (the bag must be long enough to do this), pulls the bag tight, and tapes it securely with duct tape. When he's ready to raise the mast, he cuts the plastic and tape, and there's no sticky mess on the mast and shrouds.

Mast silencer

William Cox from Rolling Meadows, Illinois, silenced the inside of his mast by filling it with Styrofoam peanuts. He used a vacuum cleaner at one end while a partner fed peanuts into the other. A screen at the vacuum end kept the peanuts in the mast. Later, when he had to do some wiring, the vacuum sucked the peanuts out in much the same manner.

Silencing nocturnal mast knock

Another super idea for silencing internal mast wires comes from John Lajeune of Marblehead, Massachusetts. A steady clanking sound was keeping him awake nights aboard his Gloucester 19, *Sarah*. The culprit was the internal wiring leading to the masthead. The next time the mast was stepped, he bought some ½-inch water-pipe insulation. Slipping it around the wires at the base of the mast, he fed it carefully up inside the extrusion. Lo and behold, no more sleepless nights. In warmer areas, a refrigeration company may carry reefer-tube insulation. It's more expensive, but the same idea.

Trailer-tongue extension

There are boat trailers that come with tongue extensions for launching, but evidently Bruce and Ginger Love's did not. After continually submerging the bed of his truck while launching *Ariella*, a 19-foot Gloucester sloop, Bruce made his own extension (see illustration).

brakes failed while parked on the ramp. Love suggests chocking the trailer wheels and even tying a safety line from trailer to truck. We recommend chocking the wheels of the vehicle as well.

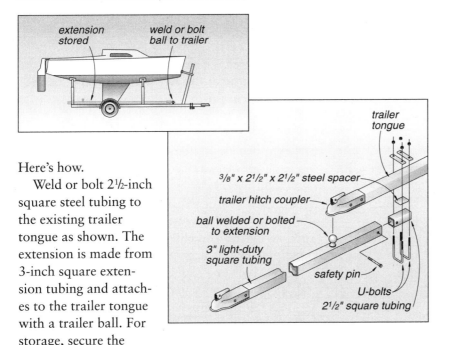

extension stored

weld or bolt ball to trailer

trailer tongue

3/8" x 2¹/2" x 2¹/2" steel spacer

trailer hitch coupler

ball welded or bolted to extension

3" light-duty square tubing

safety pin

U-bolts

2¹/2" square tubing

Here's how.

Weld or bolt 2½-inch square steel tubing to the existing trailer tongue as shown. The extension is made from 3-inch square extension tubing and attaches to the trailer tongue with a trailer ball. For storage, secure the socket of the tongue to another strategically placed trailer ball. Love claims the extension can be any length from 8 to 20 feet.

Launch-ramp bulletin boards always have photographs of submerged vehicles whose

Foolproof launching

When trailersailors launch their craft, the ramp is usually steep enough to make the task easy. Sometimes, however, even grunting and swearing fails to get the boat off the trailer. If this happens to Robert Mahar of Clearwater, Florida, he runs his winch cable through a trailer-mounted snatch block just forward of the boat's centerboard trunk and back to the boat's bow eye. A couple of turns on the winch back the boat off the trailer into the water.

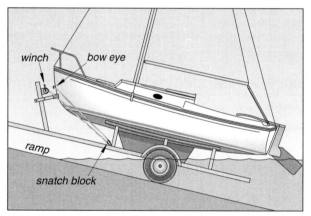

Pressurized spray

Geoffrey Coleman, who often sails with his dog aboard a Beneteau 235, *Overdue,* in Vineyard and Nantucket sounds, became fed up with gravity-fed on-deck showers. A 1½-gallon hand-pumped polyethylene garden sprayer from Sears ($20) provides "an easy way to rinse dishes or a salty dog" with pressurized spray. He adds, "Black sprayers are available if you want efficient solar heat, but boiling one quart of water and adding it to the other five will bring the temperature to just over 100 degrees Fahrenheit."

Easy electrical power

An idea for quick-and-dirty electrical power was incorporated on *Ragtop,* a San Juan 21, by cruiser/racer skipper Mike Robinson. Mike took a couple of 6-volt dry cells and wired them in series to get 12 volts. This gives him enough power for his running lights and VHF radio without the bulk and maintenance hassle of standard lead-acid batteries. This seems like a smart idea, as most small-boat running lights are nothing more than fancy (and notoriously unreliable) flashlights. A system like Mike's seems compact and reliable and could power regular 12-volt running lights.

Pole storage

"Where do you store a whisker pole on a small trailerable sailboat?" asks Steve Christensen of Midland, Michigan. His solution on *Kittywake,* his Precision 23, was to install two mast-mounted pole chocks made by Forespar. "These hold the pole on the front of the mast just off the deck, where it is always ready but not underfoot. I had to mount the pole slightly off-center, because it wouldn't clear the mast ring. If you encounter jibsheet snags, run a length of shockcord between the lower jaws of the pole and a deck-mounted padeye." To avoid turbulence when sailing upwind, he stores the pole below during club races.

Mast-stepping aid

From Norman Isler of Topsfield, Massachusetts, comes an idea that might help a trailer-sailor step his or her mast. "The most difficult task in stepping the mast on many daysailers is securing the forestay to the stemhead after the mast is raised," Isler says. His mast-stepping aid, shown below, uses a length of wooden dowel and two hooks. One hook

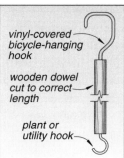

is a vinyl-covered bicycle-hanging hook, which fits around his mast. The other hook is small enough to fit into the stemhead fitting on the bow. The dowel is long enough that when the vinyl hook is around the mast and resting on the mast-mounted halyard cleats, tension is applied to the mast when the other hook is slipped into the bow fitting. With the pole in place, Isler says, he can easily secure the forestay.

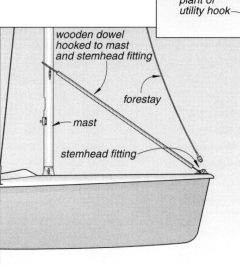

TECHNIQUES FOR CRUISERS

As we mentioned in "Modifications and Installations," one of a cruising sailor's primary concerns is where to put all the stuff you need to take with you—the longer the cruise, the more you need. There's nothing more comical (but only long after the fact) than a search for an item you know is on the boat, but you'll be damned if you can figure out where! Of course, if you live on a boat long enough, your original organization will change and, if you're anything like Nancy and me, become semi-chaotic. So if you're planning to voyage extensively or to make your boat your home, be sure to read the section devoted to creating storage—nine good ideas, some of which you might not have considered, some of which may save your sanity.

As for boathandling, have you ever tried backing into a slip when there's a crosswind or cross current? Sailboats are traditionally truant in reverse, and when you add to their normal recalcitrance the tendency—no, the determination—of the bow to fall away with the wind or current, you have the reason why most sailors enter their slips bow first. On page 140 you'll find a method ("Backing in Safely") that provides better control of the bow in such conditions. I've never tried it, and even if sailor Gannon swore on a stack of Bibles that his technique works, I'd still want to practice when nobody was around.

I had to laugh at Ron Gray's "Fishanasia" (page 167), remembering one of my own disastrous scenes in the role of fish executioner. I was trying to stab a particularly appetizing specimen with a large knife, but my bloody intentions were ineffective—I get excited when a beautiful mahi-mahi is resisting becoming part of my food chain. Eventually, however, the fish folded its tent, lifewise, and I surveyed the mess—blood all over the side deck and trunk cabin—and diesel—diesel? Running down the scuppers? In my frenzy I'd also wounded a jerry can lashed to the lifelines. Since then I've poured either rum or gin into the fish's gills, hoping to make the experience more pleasant for both of us.

Nancy has always been creative and helpful in evaluating certain types of submissions. Three that she really liked are in the following pages. For instance, did you know that dark towels will dry faster than white ones? And how about the idea for cleaning potatoes by dragging them behind the boat in a net? The third idea that Nancy swears she'll use if and when we return to trailersailer cruising is the one that tells how to make cockpit cushions out of PFDs.

Anchoring, Docking, Mooring

Piling pointers

Have you ever tied up to dock pilings at high tide, only to return to find your beloved boat suspended in mid-air? Max Elstein of Venice, California, who sails *Patience,* a 32-foot sloop, has adopted a successful way to tie up to pilings in tidal areas (see illustration). He secures the bow, stern, and spring lines to the pilings with wide bowline loops.

Using thin, chafe-resistant line cleated to the dock and tied to each bowline loop, Max can regulate the height of each loop above water level. This minimizes the effects of tidal changes, tight lines, chafe, or loose lines that allow the boat too much freedom. Beware of barnacles, however, if you hang your lines below the high-water mark. Along the same lines (sorry…), Jan Brown, who skippers a Hunter 30, keeps *Lost Shaker* off the pilings with lengths of PVC schedule 40 pipe. (The greater the distance, the thicker the pipe.)

These "dock whips" are made by threading dockline through the PVC and cleating one end of the line to the dock. Install a PVC elbow at the other end of the PVC pipe, and cleat the line to the outboard stern and bow cleats. You may have to apply chafing gear where the lines enter or exit the pipes. This system might not be strong enough in an area where a strong, onshore fetch is possible, but in protected areas (such as canals) it could be useful.

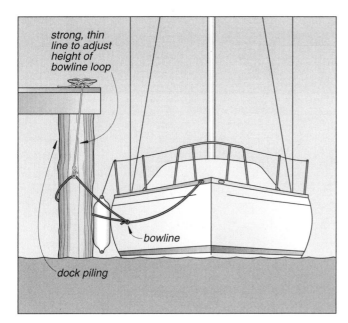

strong, thin line to adjust height of bowline loop

bowline

dock piling

Fail-safe docking

Jack Sherwood, senior editor of *Chesapeake Bay* Magazine, singlehands his 22-foot Sail-master out of Annapolis, Maryland. He claims his solo-docking method has never led to an embarrassing landing, as can so often happen when you have new crew "helping."

Jack strings a taut line across the front of the slip and along each side of the slip (see illustration). He coasts into the slip and picks up the starboard stern dock line that hangs on the outermost piling and drops it over the starboard stern cleat. This stops the boat as it nudges the bow stop line. The taut fore-and-aft lines are strung so close to the hull that they stop it from sliding off to one side. The port stern line is conveniently available, because Jack drapes it over the port fore-and-aft line when he leaves the slip (to get to it he grabs the port fore-and-aft line with a short boathook and pulls the boat over). Then he gets off the boat and retrieves the bow lines, which are permanently cleated to the dock. This system sounds great to me, particularly for lakes and saltwater areas in which tidal range is minimal.

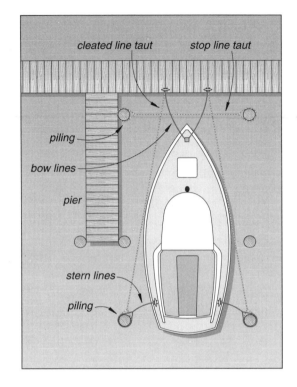

Position marks on lines

"We like to see our 11-meter S2 sloop, *Prosperity,* tied exactly in the center of her slip. To cut down on the readjustments we once had to make, we have marked the dock lines with whippings where the line touches the cleat," writes Carl A. Wohltmann of Danville, California. "It is a simple matter to cleat each line at its mark, knowing that a perfect position is guaranteed when all the lines are tied. The marks can also be made with permanent marker. Either way, they do not affect the use of the dock lines when you are tying up at other docks."

On board their 30-foot wooden cutter, *Taleisin,* Lin and Larry Pardey have used whipping markers such as these to indicate the correct positioning of the spinnaker-pole topping lift and the preferred lazyjack position. Nylon whipping thread can be felt at night and has lasted several years, so it is their first choice.

Using enough snubber

Clyde Lane, who's taking a break from cruising to work in the Marshall Islands, suggests the use of a long (20-to-40-foot) anchor snubber when anchoring. He lets out about half of the snubber and keeps the other half coiled and ready for use. In a midnight crisis he can let out or take in scope without dealing with rolling hitches, bow-roller/chock confusions, and other potential problems.

Singlehanded mooring pickup

Philippe von Hemert illustrates resourceful singlehanding. Small boats, and some lightly built larger ones, tend to fall off embarrassingly quickly when brought head-to-wind at a mooring. Philippe uses a special technique when the wind is up, he's sailing alone, and he has to pick up a mooring in his 26-foot Lubec sloop, *Chimera.* He ties a line to the samson post (you could use a bow cleat) and leads it out of the bow chock and, keeping the line outboard of everything, back to the cockpit. The cockpit end is affixed with a 1½-inch snap hook. He brings the boat alongside the mooring pennant, scoops the pennant quickly out of the water with the boathook, and clips on. The boat falls off and ultimately lies to on the extra-long pennant, which Philippe takes in at his leisure.

Docking technique

Marily Sturman writes us from Washington about a different docking method. "Aboard *French Bred,* our Beneteau First 36s7, we loop one end of a 50-foot docking line over the bow cleat, run it outside the stanchions, and then tie the bitter end to the stern cleat." To prevent fouling the prop, she takes the line about midships and brings it aboard over the stanchions. When docking, she steps off and, depending on the wind, ties off either the bow or the stern. Because of the single line, both ends of the boat remain under control. The helmsperson then steps off the boat to assist in the final tie-up, using additional lines for bow, stern, and spring. The single fore-and-aft line must be long enough to cleat at both the bow and the stern, with enough slack to reach dock cleats.

Singlehanded docking

I'm not used to the kind of slip where you dock bow-in to the pier and are held off by stern lines run to pilings. The few times I've attempted to dock this way, a gaffe of major or minor proportions has occurred, much to the amusement of whatever locals were watching. So the following idea sounds terrific, although I've not had a chance to try it.

Bud Greene, who singlehands *Wild Goose* out of Lake Worth, Florida, makes a good case. In his slip, all four lines (two stern lines tied to pilings, two bow lines tied to the dock) are adjusted to the proper length and fitted with eye splices on the boat end. Bud runs an auxiliary line from the port stern-line eye through the eyes of the port and then the starboard bow lines and back to the starboard stern-line eye (see illustration). When the auxiliary line is tight, it keeps all four docklines out of the water. "Coming into the slip," Bud says, "it's easy to grab one side or the other and tie up." Further, it appears that the auxiliary line creates a V that helps position the boat as it comes to rest in the slip.

Greene says that the auxiliary line can be fastened to the dockline eyes with bowlines or stainless-steel snaps; he uses snaps. He claims the system has worked for him for 10 years, and he wonders why everyone else doesn't do it. If the technique is as good as it looks, I could not agree more.

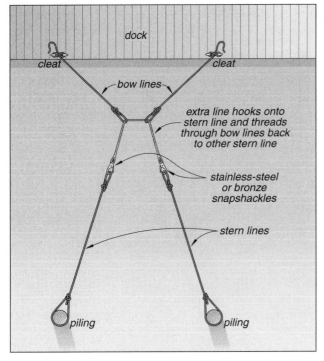

dock

cleat

cleat

bow lines

extra line hooks onto stern line and threads through bow lines back to other stern line

stainless-steel or bronze snapshackles

stern lines

piling

piling

Backing in safely

When singlehanding his Seaward 24, William Gannon of Audubon, New Jersey, found he needed a way to back into his slip against strong cross currents. He rigged permanent lines (made up of spliced together odd pieces of old rope) that go from the pilings on the exit end of his slip to the floating dock (finger pier). He spliced a snap-eye onto another old line. He then took the snap-eye and ran it through a fairlead on the bow, bringing it back along the outside of his lifelines to the cockpit.

As he begins to back into his slip, he snaps the eye onto the line near the piling that is upwind or up-current. Then, as he backs in, he pulls the other end of the line to keep the bow from falling off, controlling the bow as he works the stern toward the floating dock.

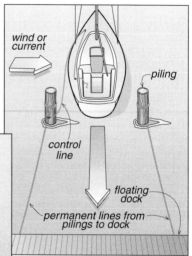

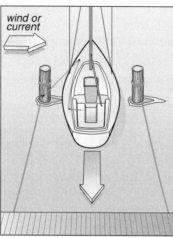

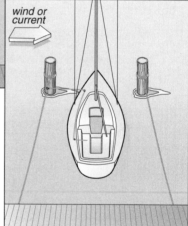

Simplified mooring pickup

A different way to ensure mooring pickup the first time around comes from New Zealand sailor D.E. Ayling. He attaches a buoy with a pennant that's the width of his boat, plus 6 feet, to the main mooring buoy. When picking up the mooring he merely steers between the buoys and picks up the one nearer to him (watch for propeller fouling).

The extra buoy serves a dual purpose; when painted black, it can be raised as a mooring signal. And should either buoy be punctured by a passing propeller, the extra buoy will save D.E. from having to dive to retrieve his mooring. He sails *Mare,* an 18-foot Kestrel of New Zealand design.

Singlehanded anchoring

Ralph Levitt often sails his Island Packet 31, *Second Love,* alone, mostly in southeastern New England. He's developed a convenient way to anchor singlehanded. Ralph mounts his anchor on a stern-pulpit bracket and leads the rode first outside everything up to the bow roller and then inside everything aft to the cockpit.

When he's in position, Ralph drops the anchor from the stern, pays out appropriate rode from the cockpit, and ties off the rode. Retrieving the anchor is equally slick. He motors up until the rode is vertical, makes the rode fast, breaks out the anchor, and hauls in the rode. As soon as he's in open water, he stows the anchor on the stern pulpit.

Cut-the-shouting headset

Bill Dabbs of Torrance, California, writes, "Kathy and I spend as many weekends as possible cruising the Channel Islands of Southern California on our Crealock 34 cutter, *Sea Dabb's*. We generally leave after work on Friday evenings, so we arrive at crowded anchorages late at night. We had problems picking our way through moorings, anchor lines, and tied-off dinghies to anchor or pick up a mooring, especially when there was no moon. We didn't want to wake people by shouting instructions, and hand signals couldn't be seen.

"We solved the problem by using a toy called My First Sony. This voice-activated transmitter/receiver headset has more than sufficient range to cover the distance between the bow and helm. It leaves both hands free to handle the windlass or helm. Instructions can be given in a normal voice regardless of wind or engine noise. The plastic housing is very sturdy, and we are still on the first set of 9-volt batteries.

"Although we look a little strange with our 'Enterprise' headsets, we have not had one husband-and-wife anchoring spat in almost two years of use."

Remote tiller steering

Al O'Neill of Newark, Delaware, has jury-rigged a device for remote steering when weighing anchor singlehanded. A common technique for breaking the anchor free when

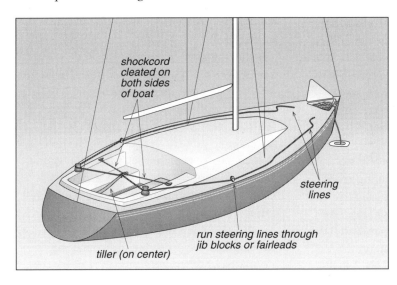

shockcord cleated on both sides of boat

steering lines

run steering lines through jib blocks or fairleads

tiller (on center)

it's firmly set is to motor forward, taking up slack as you go. When the rode is straight up and down, you take a turn around a cleat so the boat's inertia plus engine power break the anchor loose. Only then is muscle power required, as you raise the anchor from the bottom to the deck and stow it. Very simple, except when one is singlehanding in a crowded anchorage. "Spending that much time up forward, away from the helm, with the boat

under way, can be a scary experience—for you and your neighbor," says Al.

For his tiller-steered boat, Al has developed a simple way to remove a fair amount of the unwanted suspense in getting away from an anchorage. To set up the rig, he centerlines his tiller and then leads equal lengths of shockcord from the tiller to cleats on either side of the cockpit coaming. There should be enough tension in the shockcord to keep the tiller centerlined when released.

Next, he ties two longer pieces of non-elastic line to the tiller and runs them around the jib blocks (or through fairleads) on either side of the boat and forward to the bow. The resulting configuration allows Al to stand on the bow and, by pulling on the two lines, to use the tiller.

With the engine engaged or a significant way on, this method can present a degree of risk, unless the steering lines are led far enough aft to allow the tiller's full range of steering.

Creating Storage

Space saver

Julie Wood writes from Tampa, Florida, that after weekend cruising on her friend's Morgan 33, *Natasha,* she had a hard time finding a place to iron her clothes for work. Her solution was to add ironing-board material, with a pad, to the bottom of one of the boat cushions. Now ironing on the boat is as simple as turning the seat cushion over.

Cowboy-style storage

A behind-the-seat bag from a pick-up truck provides useful storage space on John Barber's *Day Dream,* a 19-foot O'Day. The bag is nylon, about 5 feet by 1 foot, and has several pockets. To secure the bag on the V-berth's port side, Barber epoxied six 2-inch-by-2-inch blocks of wood to the hull and hung the bag on cup hooks. John sails on mountain lakes near Riverton, Wyoming.

Settee storage

Many boat manufacturers provide storage areas under settees and berths that are accessible only from the top. Getting to the stored goods requires removing cushions and whatever is on them (such as people). Ralph Levitt solved this problem on *Second Love,* his Island Packet 31, by cutting access doors in the (fiberglass) sides of these lockers. Levitt bought the ready-made doors (four for $100) and four pairs of spring hinges at a chandlery. Using the doors as templates, he cut holes with a saber saw for the straight cuts and with a hole saw for neat corners; the holes are $\frac{1}{2}$ inch narrower than the dimensions of the doors. The spring hinges keep the doors tightly closed without latches. We have similar access doors with friction latches on *Red Shoes.* At sea we've been slammed by a wave, causing heavy cans to burst through the doors. Now when we go to sea, I block the doors from the inside with $\frac{1}{4}$-inch plywood that I've cut for the purpose.

Coffee table with storage

Bob Grant and his partner, Peg, needed a coffee table for their Mary Esther, Florida–based Alberg 37. Bob bought a Rubbermaid Rough Tote, which is a heavy-duty, 18-gallon plastic container. He scrounged a piece of scrap teak-and-holly sole for the lid and shaped it to match the dimensions of the container. Bob and Peg keep odds and ends inside the "coffee table" and secure it when under way with shockcords tied to a couple of small stainless-steel padeyes.

Small-boat hangups

David Jogerst sails *Ghibli,* a MacGregor 25, in Florida. He writes: "My small sailboat does not have a hanging locker, so I use the aft outboard corners of the V-berth area for clothes storage." A stainless-steel drawer pull–type handle through-bolted to the overhead turns the unused space into a place for hanging clothes. According to David, it doesn't cramp the sleeping space. My only reservation is the bolt through the overhead; without careful sealing it's a leak waiting to happen.

Book holder

Emil Gaynor of Camarillo, California, contributed this interesting solution for keeping books in place on their shelves. As he says, "There have been many schemes for holding books on a shelf; most are poor." His solution: "A piece of sail track mounted to the back of the bookshelf, a slide with a length of 1/16-inch or 1/4-inch braid, and a jam or tube cleat. This allows quick adjustment and easy removal of books with no spills or flopovers."

If you are building new shelves, the track could be made from a small piece of plate (brass or aluminum) drilled with two holes and a rabbet. This would eliminate the need for the sail track and would work just the same as Emil's slide.

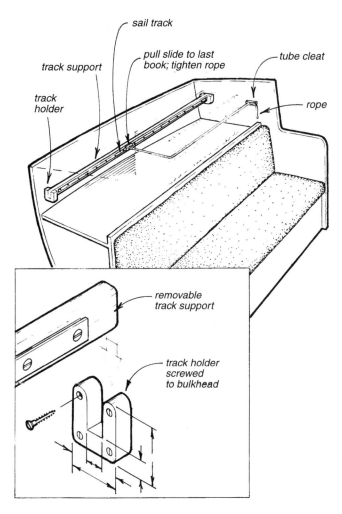

Handy storage

Judith and Anthony Kaczor, aboard *Therapy*, found storage of small items to be a problem. Their solution was to hang two conventional shoe holders (the cloth/plastic kind that can be held up by two to three small hooks at the top and can be found in discount department stores).

This clutter organizer stores lots of items, such as boat tape, cleaners, sponges, utensils, keys, wallets, registrations, licenses, and sail ties, and even holds open soda cans upright. If the shoe holders are too long to fit in the area where you want them to hang, just cut off the excess. "We installed one with two rows against the hull in our cabin area and one with four rows in the space under our cockpit."

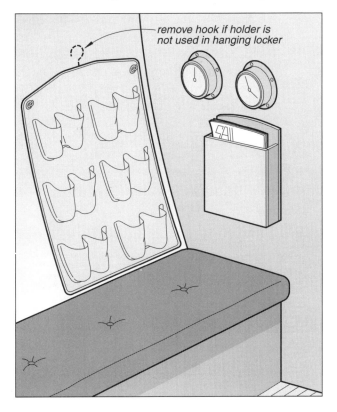

remove hook if holder is
not used in hanging locker

More storage

Jim and Carol Faulise sail their Tartan 27, *Mystic Sea,* between Nova Scotia and the Bahamas. They have extended the useful storage space of their V-berth shelves with agricultural shade screens. (This netting is available from greenhouse suppliers and works well because it won't mildew and because it remains supple in a wide temperature range.) The top of the screen is attached to the overhead with Velcro strips, and the bottom attaches to the shelf with screwed-on plastic hooks.

Carol writes, "I use two-gallon Ziploc bags to store all my clothes, separating them as one would in bureau drawers." The netting increases shelf space, and the plastic bags keep everything sorted and dry.

Boathook storage

Paul Smith aboard *Spindrift,* a sailing salmon trawler whose home port is Bodega Bay, California, finds that the backstay or a shroud is the right place to store the boathook and has come up with a simple and functional way to keep it there. He purchased a small PVC pipe-reduction fitting that is large enough to fit the head of the boathook into. Then he lashed the fitting to the backstay with heavy twine a few feet above the transom. At the other end of the boathook, he drilled a small hole in the handle and looped a piece of line through it. To secure the boathook on the backstay, Paul sets the head of the hook in the pipe fitting and loops the other end around the backstay.

Galley Innovations

No more spilled drinks

From Bob Kelly of Cleveland, Ohio, comes an idea for a beverage holder that hangs on a lifeline. Stainless-steel wire is readily available from a fence company. Bob formed his drink holders by hand around a 3-inch-diameter piece of PVC.

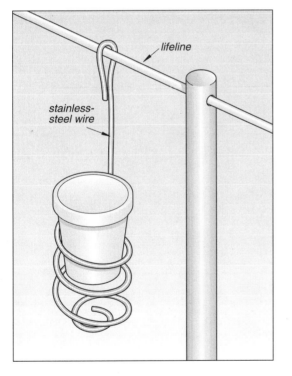

lifeline

stainless-
steel wire

A sink-mounted drink holder

For pouring drinks under sail, Herb Epstein has invented a drink holder that fits over the sink. He cut a piece of 1-inch pine into a rectangle slightly larger than his rectangular sink. He then cut four holes the size of his drink glasses into the board with a hole cutter and a sabre saw. He epoxied four strips of wood to the underside of the drink holder, one strip for each side. The strips fit snugly into the sink, and the board remains stable on top of it. Now, even when the boat is heeling, the drink maker can work without chasing sliding glasses.

Wine-glass storage

Pauline Howarth of Portsmouth, England,
has a neat idea for storing wine glasses, which

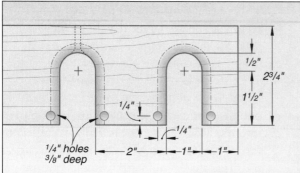

1/2"

2 3/4"

1 1/2"

1/4"

1/4"

1/4" holes
3/8" deep

2" 1" 1"

are virtually unstorable on a
boat. On her 40-foot schooner,
Barkis, she cut a 2 3/4-inch strip
of 1/2-inch plywood (see illustration) and screwed it between
two deck beams in the overhead. Rather like glass racks
used in bars, it's original by
virtue of pegs that keep the
glasses from sliding out in
rough seas. Hung upside down
by their bases, the stemmed
beauties take up no storage
space and lend a touch of elegance to the galley. On a fiberglass boat, such a rack would
work just fine mounted on a 2-inch wooden
block screwed into the wall or overhead liner.

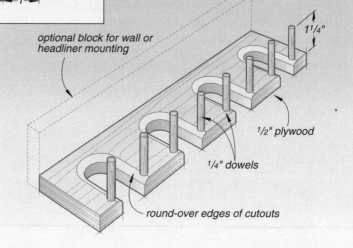

optional block for wall or
headliner mounting

1 1/4"

1/2" plywood

1/4" dowels

round-over edges of cutouts

Utensil and plate box

John Ash of Chebeague Island, Maine, has devised a handy, portable galley storage box. "I designed the box for my J/24 because I wanted to be able to offload cruising gear easily to lighten the boat for racing," he says.

He measured his utensils and plates to determine the size and shape each bin would have to be to hold everything without rattling. For the ends of the box he used ¾-inch mahogany with grooves in the front and back sections to hold the lighter plywood sides securely. Before he assembled the box, he cut an insert out of mahogany to separate the sections. He attached the insert to one side of the box with wood screws and then assembled the rest of the box around it. The front compartment is large enough to accommodate dinner plates. He wedges spatulas and serving spoons around the plates to keep them secure.

"I now own a Sabre 38 and have found that the utensil box fits perfectly just inside the aft cabin. It's held in place with a screw eye and an L-hook on the bulkhead. The box is easily accessible from the galley and is a labor saver at commissioning and decommissioning times."

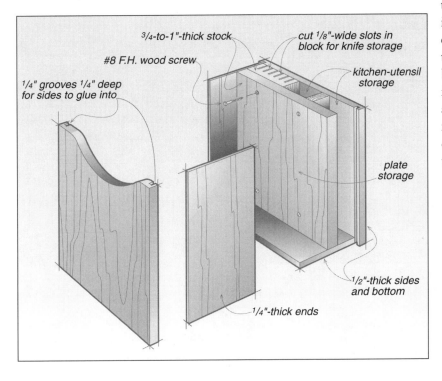

³/₄-to-1"-thick stock

cut ⅛"-wide slots in block for knife storage

#8 F.H. wood screw

kitchen-utensil storage

¼" grooves ¼" deep for sides to glue into

plate storage

½"-thick sides and bottom

¼"-thick ends

The not-so-trivial trivet

We cruisers are always looking for ways to increase storage space. A neat idea for storing cooking utensils, ladles, spatulas, and so on comes from Fred DeFoor, master of *Freebird,* a 31-foot Allmand. He searched marine catalogues but found nothing to his liking. A teak magazine rack looked promising, but it was too large, and making the necessary modifications seemed like a lot of work. DeFoor solved his dilemma by buying a teak trivet and adding three sides (see illustration). His custom unit fits the space in his galley perfectly and cost him less than $20.

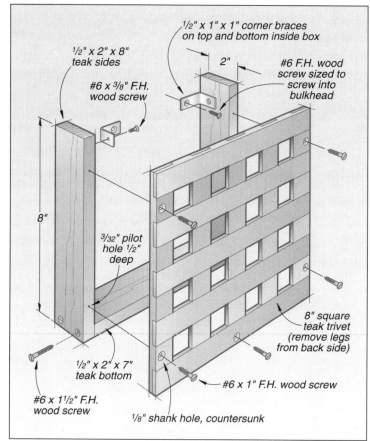

1/2" x 1" x 1" corner braces on top and bottom inside box

1/2" x 2" x 8" teak sides

2"

#6 F.H. wood screw sized to screw into bulkhead

#6 x 3/8" F.H. wood screw

8"

3/32" pilot hole 1/2" deep

8" square teak trivet (remove legs from back side)

1/2" x 2" x 7" teak bottom

#6 x 1" F.H. wood screw

#6 x 1 1/2" F.H. wood screw

1/8" shank hole, countersunk

Ice-cold water on demand

How about a faucet that produces filtered, ice-cold water? This idea was too good to put aside. A sailor who forgot to include his or her name writes, "Boats with refrigeration and a pressure water system can dispense fresh-tasting chilled water at the touch of a button. One stop at a large home center and possibly a metal fabricator can provide everything necessary (see illustration). The installation requires less room in the reefer than a 2-liter soda bottle and, most important, efficiently does away with the need to open the reefer door to rummage for a cold drink. Another advantage of this system is that you can add significantly more chlorine to the boat's water tanks to prevent the accumulation of algae and bacteria, as activated-charcoal filters remove the undesirable chlorine taste."

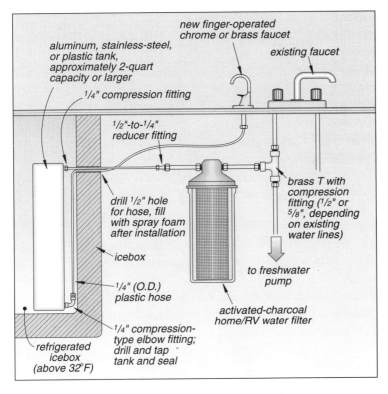

Ice for coffee?

Marvin Reynolds of Holliston, Massachusetts, and his wife, Juli Ann, both enjoy a cup of good coffee aboard their Baba 35, *Anastasia*. However, the water from their annually flushed water tanks did not give them the taste they desired.

The solution was to freeze two half-gallon containers of drinking water and use these for "ice" for the weekend. Having left one partially frozen container in the ice box, they returned the following weekend to thawed drinking water, perfect for making coffee. During the week they refroze the second container, which then provided cooling for the next trip to the boat and became the ice in the icebox. However, Marvin writes that "some containers can be frozen without cracking, others cannot. We learned it was always best to drain off a glass or two before freezing."

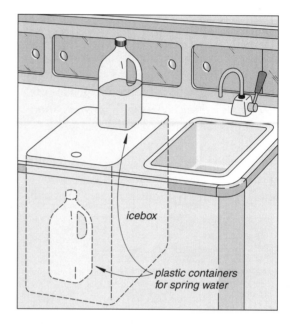

icebox

plastic containers
for spring water

No-effort potato rinsing

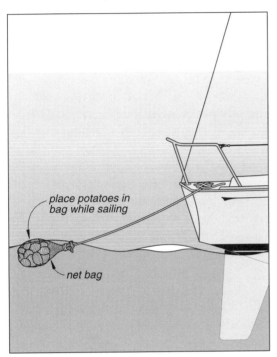

place potatoes in bag while sailing

net bag

Carl Frostell of Djursholrn, Sweden, says, "People laugh—but only once—when they see me towing a net bag full of potatoes." The fact is that the potatoes in the bag roll and scrape themselves very clean in a few minutes. The net bag is made of rather coarse cotton twine, approximately the size of an ordinary shopping bag, and has a long line to close it on top and to tow by.

Hibachi help

Gwen Bylund, who's cruising Turkish waters on *Hellem Nooh,* lights her barbecue with long piece of uncooked spaghetti. Light one end of the pasta with a match, she reports, and it will burn lustily. The added reach could save you from a painful burn.

Jar protection

Barbara Malone of *Sonnet* covers and protects jars and bottles with the tops cut off athletic socks stolen from the kids. The kids think the washing machine ate them.

No more skidding dishes

Jennifer Lindeen and her partner, Kent Holcomb, charter *October,* their Ericson 36, out of the Rio Dulce in Guatemala. To create an antiskid bottom for each dish and glass on board, Jennifer carefully squeezed silicone sealant around the bottom of each piece. She then placed the piece on a sheet of waxed paper and pressed down gently to flatten the sealant. A few hours later, she inverted the dishes and peeled away the waxed paper. "Allow 12 hours for the silicone to cure completely," she tells us. "Then, with an X-acto knife, trim away any excess sealant around the edges."

Instant ice

Terry O'Brien and Shelley Parsons left Portland, Oregon, aboard their 36-foot cutter, *Whisper,* with a small 12-volt refrigerator aboard, but no way to make ice cubes. Shelley rectified this situation by filling sealable (Ziploc-type) bags half full of water and hanging them with wooden clothes pins over the evaporator plate in the refrigerator. Terry writes: "Voila! Ice! Just the right amount to enjoy with an adult beverage as we watch the sun set in the beautiful Caribbean."

Ziploc baggy half filled with water

evaporator

12-volt refridgerator

Extending veggie life

This idea for long-distance cruisers comes from Bonaire, in the Dutch West Indies. Claire Kantor, aboard *Runaway,* recommends a product called Fresh Pak and claims it extends the life of lettuce and other veggies up to three weeks. We normally don't use submissions that tout commercial products, but this one could be such a boon to voyagers that we're including it. *Red Shoes* has ordered some, and in a few months we'll be able to report on their success. Fresh Paks are reusable, and a package of 10 costs $3. They are available from Fresh Pak Corp. (420 Lewis Wharf, Boston, MA 02110; tel. 617-782-5227).

Flatware storage

The utensil drawer in the galley of *Aquarius,* Larry Gotch's Islander 36, is deep. Rather than throw in flatware helter-skelter with cooking utensils, Larry built a partitioned flatware tray for knives, forks, and spoons that rides on rails attached to the sides of the drawer. Large items go in the bottom, flatware in the tray. Larry sails out of Darien, Connecticut.

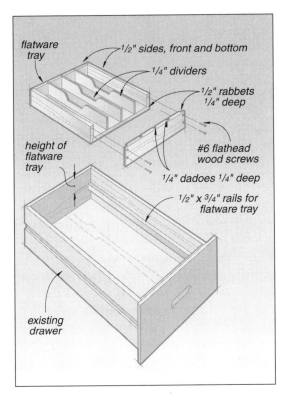

flatware tray

1/2" sides, front and bottom

1/4" dividers

1/2" rabbets 1/4" deep

height of flatware tray

#6 flathead wood screws

1/4" dadoes 1/4" deep

1/2" x 3/4" rails for flatware tray

existing drawer

Dispensing with trays

Aboard *Hellem Nooh,* a 75-foot schooner cruising in the Middle East, Gwen Bylund no longer wrestles with ice-cube trays. Instead, she fills glass or hard-plastic tumblers with a quarter-cup of water and places them in the back of the freezer. Soon she has a frosted glass with a small block of ice in the bottom. When she wants an iced drink, she tops up the glass with a beverage, and within a few minutes a giant ice cube is released—an iced drink without the hassle of ice-cube trays. If she'd sent a rack to keep the glasses upright in the freezer, we'd use it on *Red Shoes*!

Taming the gimballed stove

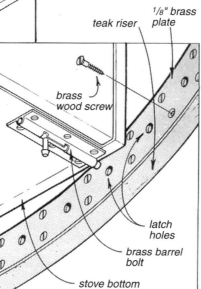

teak riser, ⅛" brass plate

brass wood screw

latch holes

brass barrel bolt

stove bottom

Cruiser Tom Linskey writes, "On our 28-foot fiberglass-hulled Bristol Channel Cutter, *freelance*, my wife, Harriet, and I found our gimballed stove to be a mixed blessing. It's great to have a level cooking surface when the boat is heeled or rolling, but in really bouncy seas the action gets out of hand. Also, in port or at sea it was a nuisance (and potentially dangerous) to have the whole stove suddenly pivot when the oven door was opened. Ideally, we wanted to be able to choose between a freely gimballing stove and one that could be locked on the level or at any angle of heel when we needed a non-swinging surface.

"To tame our gimballed stove, I bolted a brass barrel bolt (the kind with a nylon friction pad that keeps the bolt in position) onto the lower lip of the stove. I scribed the arc the stove makes when swinging onto a piece of ⅛-inch brass plate and mounted that onto a teak riser that brought the plate up next to the barrel bolt. Then I drilled and filed out latch holes in the plate for various angles of heel and on the level.

"While most times at sea we just let the stove do its own gimballing thing, in rough seas we can now lock it to approximate our angle of heel and use deep pots and pot holders if we think that is safer. In quiet ports we usually just secure it on the level, and, if the top burners are heavily freighted with boiling pots, we lock it before opening the oven door."

Cooking-alcohol container

Emma Smith of Granby, Connecticut, has found an easy way to pour stove alcohol into one of the canisters on her Origo stove. She uses a small shampoo bottle, the type found in professional hair salons, with a nozzle that can be turned up when you are ready to use it or turned down for storage. The nozzle makes it easy to pour the alcohol directly into the wick of the canister. The container is small, easier to store, and handy to reach. Place masking tape on the bottle and use a permanent marker to label the bottle as a non-hair-care product. (Do not try to fill a lit stove.)

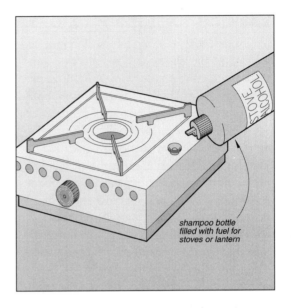

shampoo bottle filled with fuel for stoves or lantern

Easy fill for alcohol stoves

For those few remaining sailors who insist on cooking with archaic fuels, here's a tip from Matt and Donna Blaine, who sail *Grace,* an Alberg 30. Matt buys rubbing alcohol in pint-size bottles (he prefers the ones with flat sides rather than the cylindrical ones), which he says can be found on sale at three or four pints for $1. He decants the rubbing alcohol into another container, buys denatured alcohol in gallon containers, and decants that into the pint bottles. This is cheaper than buying stove fuel by the pint, and the smaller bottles make filling the stove tank neater and easier.

Ah, but what does Matt do with all that rubbing alcohol? Besides keeping some in the medicine chest, he uses it as an all-purpose cleaner—on surfaces prior to epoxying or bedding fittings; after cleaning with mineral spirits; and as a final surface prep before painting. He has also used it in the Porta-Potti on his previous boat, and in the holding tank on his present one, to kill bacteria and eliminate odors.

Fuel-gauge alternative

Bill Nichtberger, skipper of the ketch *Cetris,* has an innovative solution for those wondering how much fuel is left in a gaugeless propane or CNG bottle. To check the fuel level, slowly pour hot water down the side of the tank. The hot water causes the top layer of fuel in the tank to change from a liquid to a gas, which in turn causes the surface point of the liquid to become the coolest point on the tank exterior. Run your hand over the side of the tank. A perceptible temperature difference can be felt at the top of the remaining fuel. The hotter the water, the greater the temperature change at the liquid/gas interface.

Propane abroad

After sailing most of the way around the world aboard *Tine*, Penelope Brown was surprised to find that it was hard to get her U.S. propane bottles filled in Europe. Her "fill your own bottle" solution takes advantage of the liquid state of the fuel.

With a European fitting, an American (or British) fitting, and a 3-foot length of hydraulic hose, you can make up an easily stowed connection that allows you to buy the local gas in their bottle, fill your own bottle, and return the local bottle. The reason for hydraulic hose is that the gas is under pressure and may burst low-pressure hose.

Since the propane is in a liquid state, the law of gravity prevails. There is pressure in both tanks, so the flow will be slow. Keep the bottle to be filled below the lowest point of the bottle doing the filling. Check your progress by weighing the bottle with a fish scale from time to time. On a hot day you can speed up the process by putting the empty bottle on ice or by pouring cold water on it. As with any flammable product, care in handling is a must. Transfer the propane while ashore.

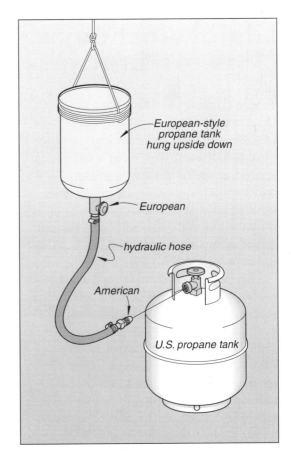

European-style propane tank hung upside down

European

hydraulic hose

American

U.S. propane tank

Life at Anchor (Tips for Cruisers)

Catching rain

On a recent passage from Samoa to Hawaii, world cruiser Gary Milici noticed that huge quantities of water were being wasted as the rain ran down his boat's mainsail and off the boom during a squall. To capture the precious liquid, he built a canvas trough that he suspended from the boom. At the lower aft end of the trough, Gary sewed in a hose barb, to which he attached a length of flexible hose.

The water-catching trough is tied off at the gooseneck and near the outhaul and is secured loosely along the length of the boom with line threaded through grommets that are sewn at intervals along the trough's edge. When it starts to rain, Gary waits for a minute or two for the salt to wash off the sails, and then he fills up his jerry cans. He says he once collected 25 gallons of water during a 3-minute squall. It sounds like a super idea for people who are good at sewing canvas and grommets, but I can see that Gary's trough might be difficult to rig on any boat whose mainsail is bent on the boom.

Bimini help

A large bimini, a luxury in tropical climes, often requires transverse rods, tubes, or poles to keep it from drooping on the sides. Most awnings require poles 10 feet long or more—a storage headache. Norman and Jeanette Ralph, who sail *Bluebonnet,* a Valiant 32, on Kentucky Lake, are planning a passagemaking retirement. They solved the storage problem by purchasing camping-tent replacement poles at a backpacking shop. These poles come in short sections that fit together to form longer lengths. Dismantled and folded together, the poles are only 30 inches long and store in a slender nylon pouch.

Awning-water collection

Stu and Judy Miller, on *Quacker Jacque III,* a Hans Christian 33, use their boat's awning to catch rainwater for drinking. A hose barb installed at the awning's lowest point provided a drainage point, but the Millers worried that debris from the awning might enter the water tanks. They solved this problem by stretching the toe of unreinforced pantyhose over the hose barb to strain the water as it enters the tanks.

Quieting transom slap

Transom slap, if you have it, can be annoying. Here's how Bruce Hughes cured the slap for his Holland 52 sloop: Thread a 25-foot length of line through a large cylindrical fender and knot the line at each end of the fender to prevent it from sliding on the line. Position the fender beneath the transom, and secure each end of the line to an aft cleat. This puts the fender between the hull and the water and breaks about 90 percent of the slapping into a soft squish.

Goof retrieval

From Chuck Coykendale of Port Clinton, Ohio, comes an idea for a simple grapnel. Take two shockcords with plastic-coated hooks and fold them so that the four hooks are together. Adjust the hooks to form a grapnel and use rigging or duct tape to hold the hooks in position; tie 20 to 30 feet of light line to the other end. The hooks are heavy enough to sink and allow recovery of fishing rods or other items lost overboard from his 18-foot catboat, *Suzanne*. Also, it's light enough to heave skyward to grab a runaway halyard.

Boater's bubble bath

"The one luxury I missed while cruising for a year aboard *Carpe Diem,* our Gulfstar 50 ketch, was a long, hot bath," writes cruiser Mary Nesbitt. For a remedy she bought a small, blow-up rubber boat at a toy store, at a cost of about $20. She slips it under the diesel-engine exhaust water while the engine's running, and when it's full she pulls it over to the gate in the lifelines and waits a few minutes for the diesel fumes to dissipate. Then she adds bubbles and perfume. "I can wash my hair by leaning back into the sea, and shaving my legs is a breeze. A quick freshwater rinse on deck is a refreshing finish. The rubber boat is also great for doing laundry on deck, and it doesn't take up too much space when deflated. While cruising on the Rio Dulce in Guatemala, I could even have hot freshwater baths. Now if I could convince my husband to float out a glass of wine…"

Hat preservation

Sun-damage consciousness has prompted most of us to wear a brimmed hat for protection, but at sea a strong breeze can blow off your favorite chapeau. To keep your hat on your head, try a system employed by Jane Mulderig from Bermuda, co-owner of *Starr Trail,* a Freedom 45. Her hat features a chin strap and a back-of-the-neck strap, so it can't blow off fore or aft. If your cloth hat doesn't come equipped that way, add pairs of closely spaced grommets on opposing sides of the brim and use one or more long shoelaces. An awl shoved carefully through the weave of a straw hat (so as not to tear the material) allows a shoestring to pass through.

Hat-on-the-head trick

Here's a good idea from Chris Cikanovich, who sails a Seafarer 30 on Chesapeake Bay with his wife, two kids, and two Labrador retrievers. He strings wine corks together with twine, piercing them the long way with a sailor's needle, and places the halo of corks around his hat brim. He's almost 100 percent sure it floats. To keep the hat from blowing away, he attaches two small alligator clips to the ends of a piece of light line, clipping one to his hat, the other to his collar.

The rat race

Gwen Bylund, who lives aboard *Hellem Nooh,* in Marmaris, Turkey, has a suggestion for sailors whose boats have rodent problems. "Try baiting your mousetrap with a glob of peanut butter," she says. Also, she claims mice won't live around the smell of mint, so a few strategically placed sprigs of the stuff might be helpful.

While sailing in Tahiti 25 years ago, Nancy and I learned another treat that rodents can't resist. Try baiting your rat trap with toasted (with a match) coconut meat. In addition to making the meat more attractive to rats, toasting eliminates any human scent.

Anti-cockroach tactic

From Ron Gray comes a recipe for "cockroach candy." Mix boric-acid powder with sweetened condensed milk to make a firm dough, and form into small, marble-size balls. At the first roach sighting, distribute the candy liberally through the boat. Don't use if you have pets or small children on board, however. Ron lives aboard *Amistad* in Puerto Vallarta, Mexico.

Clean cats afloat

Norma de Beer, who cruises on *Slipaway*, describes the problems faced by those who have a pet cat on board: "Get into a rough sea and over goes the sandbox, sand everywhere. Guests on board; oops, sand everywhere. Then there's the smell."

She solved the problem by making a spill-proof, smell-proof litter box with a plastic container, approximately 1 foot square and 6 inches deep. She used a hot needle to make holes ½ inch apart and 1½ inches up from the bottom of the container. Fishing line threaded back and forth across the inside bottom of the container makes a tennis racket-like surface. The cat sits on the fishing line; any urine goes straight through, leaving the cat's paws dry, and any droppings remain on top to be thrown out. If you attach a line to the container, it can be dropped overboard and rinsed out.

"A cat that is used to sand may need to have the sand gradually reduced while it gets used to the fishing line being in the sand," Norma adds. "Young kittens should be taught to go on a newspaper. The paper should then be put on top of the line in the box and made smaller each time until the kitten is using just the fishing line."

For times in port, a second box, with the bottom cut out, could be fixed to the toerail so it hangs outboard. This could provide your cat with an open-air toilet area and free you from having to empty the container as frequently.

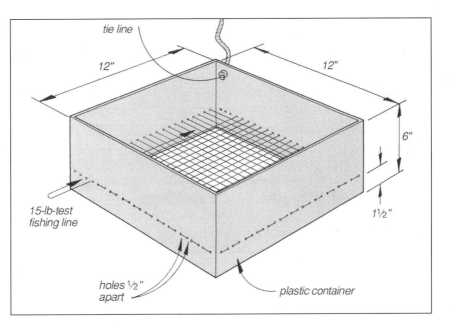

tie line

12"

12"

6"

1½"

15-lb-test fishing line

holes ½" apart

plastic container

An inspired flag halyard

Sailors often have a problem keeping proper flag-halyard tension. Too tight, and the rig's natural flexing could cause a spreader to collapse. Too loose, and the double halyard twists and tangles the flags. Pete Gustafson of Boca Raton, Florida, came up with a good idea for *Bold Response*. Using fairleads, he rigged a continuous loop through one point on the underside of the spreader midway between the mast and stay, another on the mast just below the spreader, and a third on the mast at a height convenient to reach (see illustration). The loop can be made taut, as flexing along the lower section of the mast is usually negligible. Then, using flag hooks, attach as many flags as desired. The halyard cannot tangle, and the chance of pulling the spreader out of position is greatly reduced.

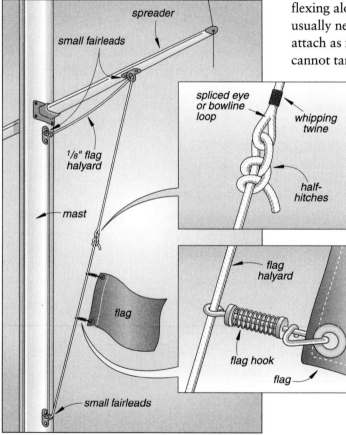

Flag care

Bill Monroe sends us a great idea from Lynn-field, Massachusetts. "To prevent flags or pennants from fraying, apply clear varnish along the edges on both sides." And, he adds, to keep the pennant mast from rattling against the mast, carefully cut a couple of holes through a tennis ball's axis, and poke the stick through it before hoisting. Bill sails *Priscilla,* a Hinckley 48.

Photo postcards

Betsy Morris, aboard *Little Haste,* a Pearson 35, came up with an idea that we like. Have your photos printed in jumbo 4-inch-by-6-inch size. She selects some non-keepers that are nevertheless quality shots and uses them as postcards. The U.S. Postal Service accepts them, and friends enjoy the personal touch.

Quick-dry towels

An idea that struck Nancy as being useful came from Marily Sturman of South Colby, Washington. She points out that black or navy-blue towels dry faster because the dark colors absorb more of the sun's heat, which causes the water to evaporate more quickly. "Even here in the cool, rainy Pacific Northwest, dark towels dry amazingly quickly with just a little sunshine." Marily also notes that they don't show as many spots.

Fishanasia

From Ron Gray, living aboard *Amistad* in Puerto Vallarta, Mexico, comes a way to deal with a large, flopping dorado or wahoo on your deck. Bludgeoning the fish with a winch handle is difficult, messy, and cruel (especially when the fish refuses to die for an inconsiderate length of time). Ron recommends keeping a squeeze bottle of 90 percent ethyl alcohol (although any bottom-shelf spirit will do in a pinch) in the tacklebox. A shot of alcohol in each gill will dispatch your catch quickly and humanely.

Navigation/ Charts

Chart magnifier

Don and Olga Casey have found a handy way to magnify charts without using a cumbersome magnifying glass. Don writes, "My eyes were never that good, and I find that a conventional magnifying glass is awkward to use and prone to falling off the chart table. Instead, I use a full sheet magnifier (a 6½-inch-by-9-inch sheet of thin plastic with amazing magnifying properties) that I found at a local bookstore for $4.50—it works much better." Don notes that this magnifier weighs next to nothing, stows flat, and can be slipped inside a chart for cockpit use. The Caseys sail *Richard Cory,* their Allied Seawind, out of Miami, Florida.

Portable chart table I

Richard Provost of Hartford, Connecticut, writes, "After several years of sailing into unfamiliar harbors with a chart stuffed under the cockpit cushion, I decided to make a permanent arrangement. I took marine-grade plywood and cut it to 24 inches by 18 inches, slightly larger than the chart kit I use. I then varnished it and attached a 22-inch by 17-inch piece of clear Lexan with two hinges on the longer side. To hold the Lexan securely over the chart, I used plastic twist-style mirror holders, which I found at the local hardware store. This table is heavy enough to stay put on the seat when I am sailing, so my chart is readily visible. On boats with larger cockpits, the table can be attached to the aft end of the cabin house."

Portable chart table II

Chris Koina, who cruises and races on a 24-foot sloop in Mooloolaba, Queensland, Australia, has designed a surface, which is both inexpensive and lightweight, for plotting and storing charts on a boat without a built-in chart table.

Chris had a sheet-metal shop roll the ends of a plate of 16-gauge aluminum to form a 17-inch-by-34-inch work surface with a curl at each end. The curl will hold up to six Admiralty charts or five U.S. Hydrographic Service charts. Chris tapes his charts into a roll to form a scroll, which he moves from one curl to the other to expose the portion he needs to reach the next point. This portable table stores inside his boat with simple clips attached to the cabintop. Turned upside down and placed across the cockpit, it serves as a cocktail table.

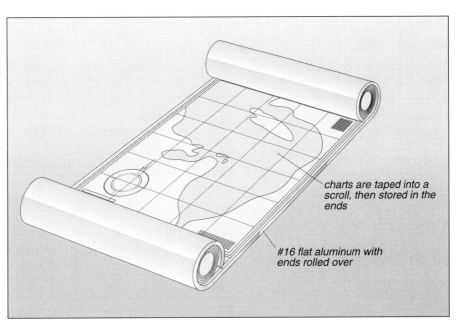

charts are taped into a
scroll, then stored in the
ends

#16 flat aluminum with
ends rolled over

Portable chart table III

Kip Bodi of Laurel Hollow, New York, built a portable chart table for his Nonsuch 26, *Motivation,* that lies over the galley stove and even serves as additional counter space when not covered with charts.

The working surface of the chart table is ⅝-inch marine-grade plywood covered with a Formica-type laminate. He attached rubber bumpers to the base for skid resistance at the end of the table that rests on the galley counter. To the other edge of the table Kip attached pieces of grooved oak flooring that fit snugly over the half-bulkhead rail. The dimensions, he says, are not important because the concept must be adapted for different-size galleys. His, however, is designed to hold standard chart kits. To finish, Kip attached a carrying handle to the front of the table for easy offloading.

Keep rolled-up charts flat

Those of us who store charts rolled up have a problem when it's time to unroll them. British Columbia sailor Linda Kuhr solved the problem aboard *Arcturus* by filling four small cloth bags with uncooked rice. The weight of the bags on the corners of a chart keep it from rolling up.

We suggest making a second set of bags and filling them with pinto beans. Then, when you're becalmed in mid-ocean and discover that the food locker is bare, you can have one last balanced meal!

Chart in the cockpit

To keep charts readily available to the helmsperson, Bill Leonard of Placida, Florida, built a shallow box with dimensions a bit bigger than those of his largest chart. He left off one side of the box and screwed it to the underside of a cockpit lazaret on his Com-Pac 19. Once installed, the box is a protected hanging shelf, safe from spray under the lazaret, and keeps charts from being blown away by a gust.

Do-it-yourself waterproof charts

John Walker sails *Rosebud,* a Com-Pac 27, on Lake Michigan. When he buys new charts he marks them with compass courses and the distances between his home port and favorite destinations and cuts them to approximately 18 inches square with rounded corners. At a picture-framing shop, he mounts a chart on either side of a foam poster board and vacuum-seals it in clear plastic. The result is a couple of waterproof charts that can be temporarily marked with a grease pencil and stored under or behind the cabin cushions.

Chart loans

Tom, Colleen, and Zoe Lyons of Ontario, Canada, have spent time on the Intracoastal Waterway aboard *Still Life.* They agree to lend their charts to friends as long as the borrower promises to make copious notes on the chart with a pencil. The Lyons have done this several times, mostly with ICW charts, and have had them returned with hundreds of marked anchorages, laundromats, dinghy docks, cheap fuel, good drinking water, and notes on car rentals, restaurants, museums, and local attractions. If you lend a chart to someone whose boat has 18-inch draft, however, the anchorages they mark for you may be less accommodating than you'd hoped.

Full-color chart markers

A quickie comes from Merry Clifford, who sails her Cape Dory 36 from Maine to Florida. To keep track of her position, she uses round, colored price stickers—red for position, yellow for anchorages. Merry sticks them to the chart with the edge folded down for easy re-sticking as *Over the Rainbow* makes its way down the Intracoastal Waterway.

Post-it Notes for chart work

Linda Stelmaszyk uses arrow-type Post-it Notes to help keep track of *Dark Star*'s position on a chart. "We navigate in some tricky channels along the Maine coast, where charts include many aids to navigation," says Linda, who sails her OC 42 out of Stonington, Maine.

Safety Issues/ Organization

Man-overboard float

George Reed of Edenton, North Carolina, dubbed his man-overboard recovery device the "Reed Retriever." To make one of your own, tightly wrap a 50-foot length of polypropylene line around a round fender as shown in the figure. Tie the bitter end to a stern cleat or rail, and leave the float accessible. If someone goes over the side, drop the fender in the water. The tuck will pull out and the line will stream out behind the boat, free of tangles. The larger the float, the greater the device's buoyancy. Use polypropylene line because it floats.

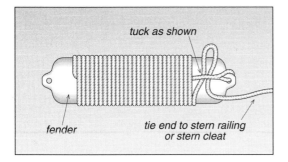

tuck as shown

fender

tie end to stern railing or stern cleat

Emergency steering

Donald Launer, skipper of *Delphinus*, a 39-foot Lazy Jack schooner designed by Ted Brewer, suggests that in certain circumstances, drilling a hole in your rudder might save the boat. Donald drilled a hole in the upper, aft corner of his rudder so that in the event of an catastrophic steering failure, a line can be passed through the hole, knotted on each side of the hole, and brought up on deck on the port and starboard sides.

With a wooden rudder, nothing more has to be done than drilling the hole and applying bottom paint to the bare wood. For fiberglass rudders with a wood core, it would be wise to dig out some of the core and fill it with a resin/glass mix before applying bottom paint. The edges of the hole should be beveled and sanded smooth to eliminate any sharp edges. On *Delphinus*, which sails out of Forked River, New Jersey, the hole is just below the waterline and in an emergency could be reached by dinghy.

Singlehander's last-chance lanyard

D.J. Young of Chorleywood, England, calls this safety line a "last-chance lanyard." He says, "Whenever I am sailing singlehanded I trail a line over the stern. It started as a trailed warp of about 15 feet, but over the years I have added various improvements."

First he put a length of rubber tube over the end loop to keep the loop always open, making it easier to grab. Then he added a connector in the middle of the line to make it easier to haul oneself along it back to the boat. He had never seen his method of making a connector in the middle of a line published before: It's made by tying two lengths of rope together using two bowlines, leaving a loop of any desired size between each of the knots. D.J. writes: "The knots keep the connector spread open, whereas a spliced loop in the middle of a line closes up."

His boat has a stern boarding ladder that folds down from the stern pulpit, so he ties a lanyard to a rung so that the ladder falls into the down position if the lanyard is pulled. This means, of course, that the ladder must not be hooked into the stern pulpit while sailing. "I thought this arrangement could be dangerous if I were to fall against it, so I rigged up a short length of line across the gap in the stern pulpit and pulled it tight with a

pelican hook. To keep the ladder in place I tied it to this short line with a breakable piece of twine."

Finally, he writes, "In order to disengage the autopilot (and hopefully have the boat round up into the wind and slow down), I hook a small line over the autopilot pin on the tiller so that, if the line is jerked, it will pull the push-pull arm off the pin."

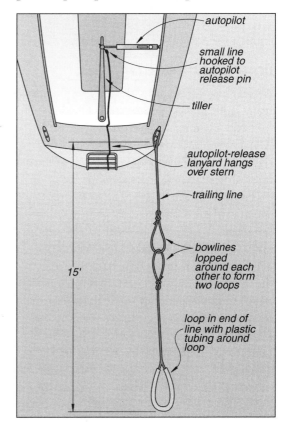

autopilot

small line hooked to autopilot release pin

tiller

autopilot-release lanyard hangs over stern

trailing line

bowlines lopped around each other to form two loops

loop in end of line with plastic tubing around loop

15'

Impromptu engine cooling

Roger Zinn was approaching his Marina del Rey, California, slip in his 36-foot Magellan ketch, *Mary Ann,* when the engine overheated because of a malfunctioning water pump. He used a spare piece of hose and two hose clamps to connect the galley faucet to the engine fitting at the water pump. The pressure water system cooled the engine long enough for *Mary Ann* to limp into her slip.

Low-cost security

A great idea for a cheap alarm system comes from Tim Kiurski, who recently sailed his 38-foot cutter, *Cloud Nine,* from Michigan to Alabama via the inland waterways. Tim rigged a 120-decibel personal alarm, available in most Sharper Image–type catalogues, for his companionway hatch. The beauty of this alarm is that it's activated by pulling a pin (attached to a lanyard) out of the alarm housing, sort of like a grenade. He attaches the alarm housing to one of the hatchboards and the lanyard to the sliding hatch with an eye-bolt, leaving just enough slack in the lanyard to allow installation of the top hatchboard. He claims this won't deter a hardcore thief, but it might scare away his apprentice.

Rudder-loss protection

When the rudder quadrant on *Limerick,* Mike LaVecchia's Hunter 33, needed repair, he found a way to keep the rudderpost from sliding out of the gland. His solution was to place a bosun's chair under the rudder and secure the chair with lines to topside cleats (see illustration). He was then able to remove the quadrant from the rudderpost without fear of losing the rudder. Mike sails on Vermont's Lake Champlain.

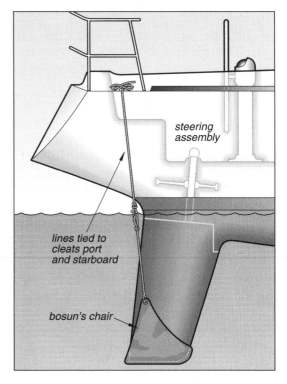

steering assembly

lines tied to cleats port and starboard

bosun's chair

PFD cushions

Anchored off a golden beach in the clear waters of a tropical cove, we enjoyed drinks with Earl Gill and Barbara Malone aboard *Sonnet*. Seeing some of their ideas, we suggested that they submit them and they agreed, provided we send payment to the Tristan Jones fund. Nancy immediately latched onto an idea of Barbara's. PFDs are bulky, and unless she falls overboard and profits from one, she'll always begrudge them locker space. Barbara freed up her locker by making a canvas slipcover with a Velcro closure for each PFD. What were once a storage problem have become attractive cockpit cushions.

Cockpit-locker lock

A unique idea for securing a vessel with a single padlock comes to us from Ian Ellis, who owns a Montgomery 17 named *Blue Skies*. He leads a line from the inside of his cockpit-locker hatch to a horn cleat inside the cabin (see illustration). Before locking the main hatch, he secures the line (and the hatch) in the horn cleat. He can then lock his boat using just one padlock for the companionway hatch.

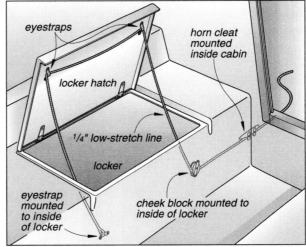

eyestraps

horn cleat mounted inside cabin

locker hatch

¼" low-stretch line

locker

eyestrap mounted to inside of locker

cheek block mounted to inside of locker

It's a lock

Just as it is in the "real world," thievery can be a problem for cruisers, so it's good general policy to lock everything on your boat. Monty Morris, who cruises *Little Haste,* a Pearson 35, in the Caribbean, locks his hatches, lazarets, outboard engine, dinghy, and bicycles whenever he leaves his boat. This means he needs seven padlocks, but since he didn't want to carry seven different keys and he found set-it-yourself combination locks to be too expensive, he special-ordered seven padlocks that use the same key. Morris claims this special order simplified his life and can be arranged through most hardware stores.

Organization map

Another far-more-organized-than-I reader, Lowell Holmes of Wichita, Kansas, came up with this idea to find stuff on his Nor'sea 27, *Taupou.* He glued a diagram of his boat on one side of a piece of plywood. He labeled each locker with a letter and created a legend on the side of the diagram, leaving space to describe the contents of the lockers. He glued a piece of Plexiglas over the plywood and used a grease pencil to note the lockers' contents. As the contents of the lockers change he can easily relabel the diagram.

On *Red Shoes,* the thought of trying to describe the contents of our quarterberth, hanging locker, or lazarets is daunting. I'd probably end up scrawling "misc. stuff." But if this works for you…

Universal status board

Would you like to have the tides for the week always in view? What about horn signals for navigating the Intracoastal Waterway? Radio frequencies for weather? To keep this vital information handy, Ken Klein of Crawfordville, Florida, made a status board for *Sun Seeker,* his Morgan Out Island 41. He took a ¼-inch-by-5-inch-by-24-inch piece of Plexiglas and glued a ⅛-inch strip of wood along one long side and both short sides to create a frame. Klein mounted the Plexiglas with wood glue to an available bulkhead. He then cut posterboard to fit the frame and created templates that slide behind the Plexiglas. Ken's standard template is divided into three panels for tidal, weather, and radio-frequency information. He uses a grease pencil to write information on the Plexiglas, which can be erased and rewritten as needed.

A viable status board can be of nearly any size, and the templates can be divided into as many sections as desired. For easy removal, be sure to make the slide-in templates slightly taller than the plexiglass compartment.

Log plus

Keeping a log is something most skippers do, but Carolyn Corbett, who sails *Bifrost,* a Morgan 41, has developed a social log for sailors. Her three-ring binder contains several sections: frequently called phone numbers, address lists, business cards covered with clear plastic, and details concerning ports. "The most vital section," says Carolyn, "is a listing of every boat we meet, the names of the crew, and a brief note to jog our memory for the next encounter."

This kind of log requires the kind of consistency that many kick-back-and-relax cruisers might not have. But for those who can develop a routine for making entries, it would be very useful.

Organization solution

Matt Blaine, a sailor out of Laurel, Delaware, uses small tackle boxes, each a different color, for storing and keeping track of stuff on board. He keeps an eye open for sales, flea markets, and yard sales at which to find tackle boxes in different colors. On *Grace,* Matt's Alberg 30, orange is for medical supplies; gray for small tools; dark blue for wrenches; yellow for fasteners, cotter pins, and the like; light blue for extra blocks and shackles; brown for nylon ties, tape, and tubes of sealants; aluminum for rigging tools and supplies; and tan for—you guessed it—fishing gear. He plans to acquire one more tackle box for small engine parts.

Organizing boat papers

Sharon Upton from Vancouver, British Columbia, spent 10 years building an MC 39. Far more organized than most of us, Sharon suggests buying three-ring binders and clear, top-loading report covers for all boat expenses. She uses these transparent pockets for all documents pertaining to ship's gear and maintenance instructions, receipts, labels removed from varnish cans, and repair or warranty receipts and records. She recently found her system worth its weight in Monel when a depthsounder caused problems and the manufacturer wanted to see records of her work. Isn't it true that one of the most difficult tasks in boating is keeping an inventory of the what and where of stuff on board? Sharon's suggestion is a simple solution to at least a part of the problem.

Dinghy Works

Dinghy boarding ladder

For hulls with low to average freeboard, this single-step ladder for boarding from the dinghy makes good sense. Larry Watkins, who sails *Fair Adventure,* a Catalina 30, out of Long Beach, California, came up with the idea. The step (see illustration) is made of ³/₄-inch marine plywood, though he says teak would be classier. The sides are attached with bronze or stainless-steel hinges. The step is hung from ½-inch nylon lines, which have hooks that attach to the genoa-track cars or the aluminum toerail.

The step folds nearly flat for easy storage. A nice touch: Larry glued scrap line to the back of the step to protect the hull. If you like this idea but aren't up to the construction, a similar step is available from the Edson Corporation (tel. 508-995-9711).

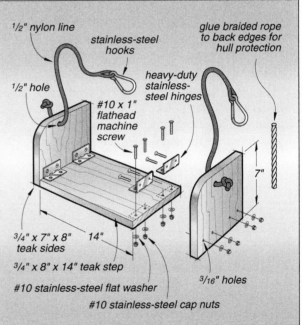

1/2" nylon line

stainless-steel hooks

glue braided rope to back edges for hull protection

1/2" hole

heavy-duty stainless-steel hinges

#10 x 1" flathead machine screw

7"

3/4" x 7" x 8" teak sides

14"

3/4" x 8" x 14" teak step

#10 stainless-steel flat washer

3/16" holes

#10 stainless-steel cap nuts

Outboard dolly

Robert Dougherty, who sails a "nameless" Santana 21 out of Palm Harbor, Florida, has found an inexpensive way to put wheels on his auxiliary outboard motor. At a flea market he purchased an old hand utility cart for $5. He attached a short piece of two-by-four with U-bolts at the top of the cart to act as the outboard's mounting bracket. When he wants to move his outboard, he simply clamps it down onto the bracket and wheels the motor away.

When he wants to flush out the motor, he slips a 6-gallon plastic bucket (which grocery stores often have) under the propeller while the motor is hanging from the transporter, fills the bucket with fresh water, and starts it up.

The cart also makes a dandy frame on which to store the motor in the garage. After running fresh water through the motor, he wheels it into place and tosses a cover over it.

Eliminate black marks

The little rubber tips on inflatables often leave black marks not only on the topside of the owner's boat, but also on the topsides of boats he visits. Dave Nof of Saint Petersburg, Florida, solved this problem: "Grind down the tips of the dinghy to a somewhat smooth finish (I used a belt sander). Be careful not to touch the main tubes while you are grinding. Clean the area and apply adhesive from your inflatable patching kit. Cut some material just a bit larger than needed and follow the directions for patching a hole. The next day trim excess material off the cover-up patch and clean excess glue off the tubes with acetone. These patches will relieve you from the job of scrubbing black marks from your sailboat's hull."

Outboard hoist

David Comerzan, aboard the ketch *Misty*, has found that lifting an 84-pound outboard 5 feet up onto the deck can be quite a challenge. "I quickly saw the advantage of using the mizzenboom with a block-and-tackle as a kind of crane," he says. "I stitched a sling of 1-inch nylon webbing to snugly fit the head of the outboard. I attached an eyebolt at the end of the boom to which I hook the block-and-tackle. Once attached to the outboard, the system easily pulls the outboard up and over the deck."

For sloops and cutters, the mainboom and a preventer can also be used. In all cases, be sure the topping lift is extra sturdy to support the weight of the outboard.

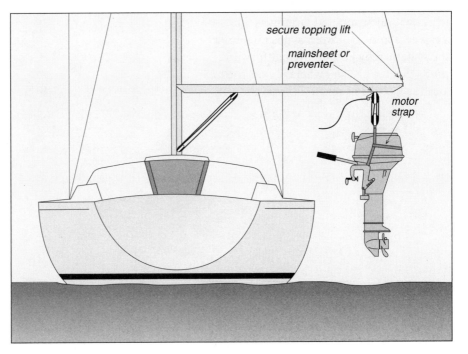

secure topping lift

mainsheet or preventer

motor strap

Primary care for inflatables

William Beery, who sails *Sea Urchin*, a Hunter 34, out of Darien, Connecticut, shares some ideas that increase an inflatable's utility. Noting that most people enter (or tumble into) the dinghy at the bow, he installed a covered 5-gallon plastic bucket. Tied in place to strapping eyes affixed to the removable wooden floorboard, the bucket provides a secure step, as well as dry storage for running lights, a flashlight, and flares. For a seat he added an oak board across the tubes, lashed in place to the handhold grommets. He used strap eyes to tie the external gas tank under the seat, thereby keeping weight forward, protecting the gas line where it exits the tank, and shading the plastic tank from the sun.

Just for kicks

Emil Gaynor of Camarillo, California, skippers a Cal 2-46. Tired of guests accidentally kicking the valve of his inflatable's V'd bottom and, eventually, damaging it, he epoxied a teak ring to the floorboard through which the valve protrudes. The raised ring has a hole the same size as the hole in the floorboard and is about 1 inch wide. The cost of valve salvation? A bit of teak, a tad of epoxy, and yet one more thing to varnish.

Dollar dinghy drain

George Reed, owner of *Echo,* a Nonsuch 30 he sails on North Carolina's Albemarle Sound, sent in an idea for a virtual perpetual-motion machine. Evidently Reed's inflatable tender takes on water under tow, which led to this drainage system for inflatable dinghies only. Reed began by filling his tender with a typical load (driver, outboard, and gas tank) and marking the waterline on the transom. He cut a hole in the transom above the water-line and inserted PVC piping and rubber hose as shown in the illustration. The flexible hose, cut on a bias, is below the waterline, where, Reed says, it will develop suc-tion and start siphoning water out of the tender. A word of caution: If the transom hole is drilled too low, the tender may take on water. We haven't had a chance to test this, but if it doesn't work, all you'll have spent is a dollar or so.

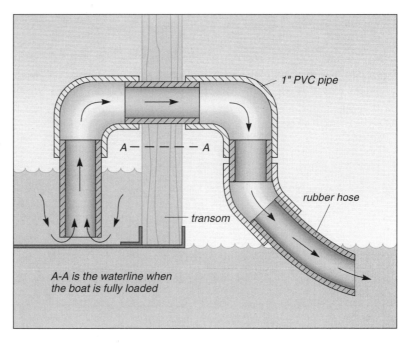

1" PVC pipe

A — — — — A

rubber hose

transom

A-A is the waterline when the boat is fully loaded

Dinghy control

Tom Tursi of Horsham, Pennsylvania, finds his dinghy has a mind of its own. "No matter what I want it to do, it always does the opposite, and when I think it's going to do the opposite, it finds something else to do." His solution is simplicity itself: Use a double painter, one secured to each stern cleat, run it through the dinghy's bow ring, and adjust the length depending on the situation.

When under sail, allow a generous length of painter for trailing a hard dinghy. You'll find that the dinghy trails better with two painters, not to mention the added security of having an extra line. When you're docking or anchored for the night, an inflatable dinghy can be snugged in tight to the transom with both painters. If you lift the bow against the transom and tie it off, your inflatable will ride quietly through the night.

Tame that towed dinghy

A good dinghy-towing idea comes from Bernard Wideman, who sails *Chimo*, his Sabre 28, out of Casco Bay, Maine. Bernard fastens a shockcord across a bight in his dinghy painter. As the dinghy exerts more drag, the shockcord stretches until the painter takes the full load. Thus the shockcord acts as a damper and keeps the dinghy from jerking the painter and deck cleat.

Wideman credits the idea to his sailing partner, Bob Mongeon. We tried this on *Red Shoes* last month while towing our hard-bottomed inflatable dinghy in 25 to 30 knots of wind. A sizable chop caused severe dinghy slaloming. The shockcord worked, but we destroyed a 2-foot length of $\frac{3}{8}$-inch shockcord in the process. Methinks an anchor snubber would be more durable while still providing damping.

Towing rudder for inflatable dinghies

This is an interesting idea for owners of keel-less inflatables. Kim Downing of Traverse City, Michigan, found that his roll-up inflatable spun about when towed, particularly in moderate-to-rough seas. After breaking one towing bridle, he designed a small and easily removed rudder that can be attached to the inflatable's transom for towing. The rudder is mounted and removed with bolts and wing nuts (see illustration). From a *Red Shoes* perspective, this rudder might be good for rowing stability as well.

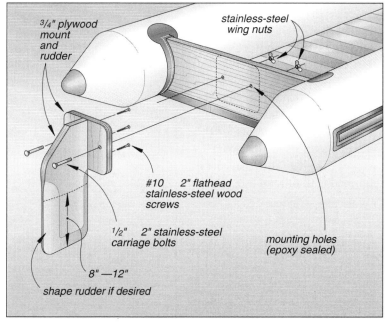

3/4" plywood
mount
and
rudder

stainless-steel
wing nuts

#10   2" flathead
stainless-steel wood
screws

1/2"   2" stainless-steel
carriage bolts

mounting holes
(epoxy sealed)

8" —12"

shape rudder if desired

Dinghy oar rack

Pat and Paul Janson, who cruise the Chesapeake on their Bristol 29.9, *Ardea,* deflate their small inflatable dinghy when they aren't using it and stow it in its bag. Paul found that packing the oars and wooden seat in the same bag made storing the dinghy in a cockpit locker difficult. He also worried that sharp edges and corners of the collapsible oars would cause wear and tear on both the dinghy and the bag. So he devised the two-part rack shown in the illustration and doubled the usefulness of his hanging locker by screwing the rack inside against a bulkhead. A shockcord restraint keeps the oars from rattling. The seat slips into the corner behind the oar rack. Angling the cutouts for the blades makes the rack as compact as possible. The total cost is minimal, and only simple tools are needed.

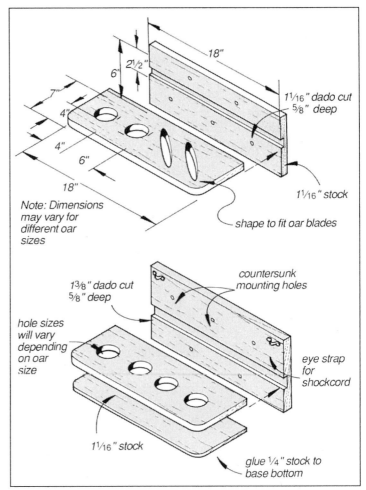

18"

2½"

6"

7"

4"

4"

6"

18"

1¹⁄₁₆" dado cut ⁵⁄₈" deep

1¹⁄₁₆" stock

shape to fit oar blades

Note: Dimensions may vary for different oar sizes

1³⁄₈" dado cut ⁵⁄₈" deep

countersunk mounting holes

hole sizes will vary depending on oar size

eye strap for shockcord

1¹⁄₁₆" stock

glue ¼" stock to base bottom

Dinghy fenders

David Buckman of Gilford, New Hampshire, has found a do-it-yourself alternative to costly dinghy-fender material. He purchased a package of ½-inch foam pipe insulation (the

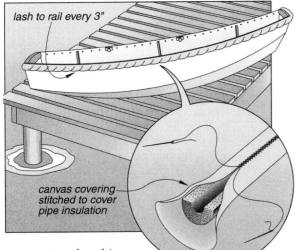

lash to rail every 3"

canvas covering stitched to cover pipe insulation

non-water-absorbing, closed-cell variety) and 2 yards of white canvas; the total cost was $19.

He writes: "I sliced the pipe insulation in half (it was already slit on one side) and cut a length of canvas wide enough to wrap around the foam and allow the cut edge of the fabric to be tucked under, to eliminate exposed-edge fraying." Then with a needle in hand and a double line of polyester thread, he spent two hours sewing it together. He taped the foam

together and, when he came to the end of the first 6-foot length of canvas covering, he overlapped the next length a couple of inches and sewed them together.

Running a steam iron over the back seam when it was finished snugged the canvas up nicely. All that remained was to lace it to the gunwale of the dinghy (at 3-inch intervals) with whipping twine. David writes, "It looks good, and because this foam is a bit softer than the store-bought stuff, it works better, too." He says he's got enough canvas left over to re-cover the fenders three or four times.

INDEX

A

alarm system, low-cost, 174
alcohol. *See* stove fuel
anchor, weighing, singlehanded, 143
anchor buoy, tether for, 46
anchoring: cut-the-shouting headset, 142; singlehanded, 141
anchor light, 45
anchor rode/chain: mounted on stern pulpit, 141; removable locker, 52; stopper, 50
anchors/ground tackle: bowsprit protection from, 48; storage, 48, 50, 52, 53, 54
anchor snubber: bridle, 49; long, 137
anti-fouling paint: ablative, 87; on propeller, 87
anti-skid: for cooler, 128; for dishes/glassware, 155; for objects on tables/counters, 120, 123; for outboard fuel tank, 125
autopilot: case for, 40; lines to disengage, 173; tiller for, 43
awning: pole storage, 162; as rain catcher, 162

B

bag, storage. *See* storage bag
bathtub, rubber boat as, 163
batteries, adding water to, 18, 27
berth: cockpit grate as, 128; side storage access, 144

bilge, draining, 125
bimini pole storage, 162
binnacle cover, 75
bird droppings, barriers/deterrents, 54, 55, 56, 57
bleach, from swimming-pool chlorinating tablets, 2
block: fiddle, 101; grooved teak, 98
boarding ladder/steps: for dinghies, 179, 182; for boats with high freeboard, 45; safety lanyard from, 173
boat covers: framework for, 28; tie-downs, 1, 29, 30
boathook storage, 148
boat name, vinyl lettering, 60
boat papers, storage/organizing, 178
bolts, threading nuts in cramped areas, 8, 9
bookshelves, sailtrack holder for, 146
boom, main: asymmetrical support, 83; crutch, 84; gallows, 86; outboard hoist, 181; topping lift controls, 95, 96, 97
bosun's chair, 93; for securing rudder, 174; stirrups for, 94
bottom: anti-fouling paint, 87; cleaning/scrubbing, 58; sanding, 59
bow pulpit, dropping-free bird perch, 57
bowsprit protection, 48

brass, polishing, 18
breaker panel, wiring for navigation lights, 42
bronze, polishing, 18

C

cables, replacing, 15
cam cleat, 101, 126
canvas: cockpit cover, 85; rain catcher, 162; sail-cover closures, 108; windscoop, 85
cat's litter box, 165
centerboard, stuck, pusher for, 117
chafing gear: for dock lines, 47, 48; fire hose as, 45; for lifelines, 65; for shrouds, 100
charts: lending, 171; magnifier, 168; position markers 171; storage, 169, 170; waterproof, 171
chart tables, 168, 169, 170
chlorine bleach, from swimming-pool chlorinating tablets, 2
cleaning: bottom, 58; computer diskettes, 42; copper washers, 24; fender, 14; fiberglass topsides, 14; glass, 14; head, 3, 160; Lexan/Plexiglas, 74, 75; mold/mildew, 42; nylon scrubbers for, 14; rubbing alcohol for, 160; tape residue, 14
cleats: midship, for spring lines, 103; preventing hangups, 100; for shrouds, 103; substitute for, 97

clevis rings, alternative to cotter pins on turnbuckles, 90

clothes: hats, 164; ironing, 144; laundering, 164; storage, 145, 148

cockpit: canvas cover, 85; chart storage, 168, 169, 170; clearing space, 43; cushions, 78, 121, 175; dodger guard, 86; drink holders, 73; sleeping in, 128; tables for, 69, 70, 71, 72, 168, 169

cockpit sole, wood grate as berth, 128

cockroaches, 164

coffee water, 154

color-coding: storing small items, 178; tools, 20, 178

companionway hatch: drink holder, 73; hatchboard stowage, 118, 119; instrument mount, 35, 175; locking, 62; plastic cover, 74; rejuvenating Lexan/Plexiglas windows, 120; screens, 33, 61, 62; step, 128

compass: cover for, 75; error, 36; gasket for, 8; wiring light, 42

computer diskettes, storage/mildew, 42

cooler: anti-skid for, 128; as companionway step, 128

cotter pins, using clevis rings instead of, 90

curtains, alternatives to, 77

cushion, boat: anti-skid for, 121; cover for, 78; as ironing board, 144; PFD as, 175

cutless bearing, replacing, 26

D

daysailers, trailersailing tips, 126 - 133

deck: foredeck jib net, 107; installing through-deck fittings, 61

deck hardware, installing, 61

deodorants for head, 6

depthsounder transducer mount, drill-free, 37

diesel fuel, avoiding spills, 19

dimples, to lock any nut in place, 8

dinghy, hard: boarding step/ladder, 179, 182; controlling/ towing, 184; fenders, 187

dinghy, inflatable: black marks from valves, 180; controlling/towing, 184, 185; drain, 183; seat, 182; securing gas tank, 182; boarding step/ladder, 179, 182; stowage, 182, 186; valve protection, 182

dishes/plates: anti-skid, 155; storage, 151

diskettes, computer, storage/mildew, 42

docking: fenders, 50; singlehanded, 136, 139; single-line technique, 138. *See also* slip

dock lines: chafe protection, 47, 48, 135; line hangers, 90; permanent, 140; position marks on, 137; single fore-and-aft line, 138; for singlehanded docking, 136, 139; spring-line cleats, 103; storage rack, 80; tie-ups/pilings, 135

dodger, cockpit, guard for, 86

drifter, repair patch, 108

drink holders: cockpit/companionway, 73; galley sink, 149; lifelines, 149

E

electrical connections, protection for, 12

electrical panel, wiring for navigation lights, 42

electricity: easy power source, 131

engine: adding coolant/transmission fluid, 27; clearing intake strainer, 7; freshwater flushing, 25, 32; improvised cooling system, 174; oil/filter changes, 20, 21, 22, 23, 24; water pump malfunction, 174; winterizing, 32

engine, outboard: dolly for, 180; flushing, 180; hoist for, 181; quick shifter, 127; starter, 125; storage, 180; tilting aid, 126

epoxy, mixing small amounts, 88

eyebolts, alternative to padeyes, 24

F

fender: as anchor buoy, 46; board for, 51; cleaning, 14; for dinghy, 187; as man-overboard float, 172; for quieting transom slap, 163; rigging, 50

filter, fuel, changing, 19

filter, oil, changing, 20, 22, 24

filter, water, carbon, 2

fingers, protection of, while sanding, 59

fingernail polish, to protect electrical connections, 12

fish, killing, 134, 167

flags: care, 167; halyard tension, 166

flopper stopper, homemade, 44

fluids, bottle for refilling, 27

foredeck netting: lacing jib net, 107; tensioning, 67

forepeak divider, 53

forestay: protection, 30; securing aid, 133

friends, social log of, 177

fuel, diesel, avoiding spills, 19

fuel filters, changing/priming, 19

fuel lines: bleeding/servicing, 19, 20, 24; cleaning washers, 24

fuel tank, anti-skid for (outboard), 125

funnel, oil, 22

G

galley: anti-skid, 120, 123, 155; dish/utensil storage, 150, 151, 152, 155, 157; draining sink, 125; drink holders, 73, 149, 155; drinking water, 153, 154; ice/icebox, 154, 156, 157; glassware protection/storage, 149, 150, 155; vegetable storage, 156; stove fuel, 159, 160, 161; stoves/grills, 155, 158; stovetop chart table, 170

gasket, emergency, 8

gas tanks, anti-skid for, 125

gelcoat: cleaning, 14; repair, 13

genoa track, alternative, 106

glass, cleaning, 14

glassware: anti-skid for, 155; protection/storage, 149, 150, 155

GPS: mount for, 35; waterproofing, 35

graphics, custom vinyl lettering, 60

grapnel, simple, 163

grills, lighting, 155

grommets, alternative, 1, 29

gybe preventer, 94

H

halyards: attachment, 97; flag/pennant, 166; preventing wrap, 102; retrieval, 163

hand-hold covers, 84

hat: floatable, 164; securing, 164

hatch: rejuvenating Lexan/Plexiglas windows, 120; screens for, 33, 61, 62; single-padlock locking system, 175

hatchboards, stowage, 118, 119

head: cleaning, 3, 160; deodorizing, 5, 6, 160; pumping dry, 1

headsails. *See* drifter; genoa track; jib, roller-furling; spinnaker

headset, transmitter/receiver: for anchoring/mooring communications, 142

heater strip, 122

heaving line, 92

helm: seat, 79; stowage underneath, 80

holding tank: clearing blockages, 4; pumpout aid, 4, 5

hooks, to aid mast-stepping, 133

hose: clearing, 4; cutting, 10; deodorizing intake hose, 5; see-through, 5

hot-water bottle, for refilling fluids, 27

hull, fiberglass: cleaning topsides, 14; scrubbing bottom, 58

I

ice: instant ice cubes, 156, 157; thawed for drinking/coffee water, 154

icebox drains, 124

indicator light, for water pump, 39

instrument covers, 75, 76

instrument panel: hinged, 34; Lexan/Plexiglas covers, 75, 76

ironing board, boat cushion as, 144

J

jib: folding/flaking, 116; whisker pole for, 113

jib, roller-furling: adjusting sheet lead, 106; protection, 30; preventing halyard wrap, 102; reefing aid, 101; security for, 106

jib net, lacing, 107

jibsheet, controlling, 106

K

knotmeter transducer tube, 36

knots: securing with glue, 87; in synthetic rope, securing, 87. *See also* ropework

L

launching, from trailer: tips, 130, 131; tongue extension, 130

laundry: drying towels, 167; rubber boat laundry tub, 163

lazaret lid holder, 78

lettering, custom vinyl, 60

Lexan: chart table, 168; cleaning/polishing, 74, 120; instrument-panel protection, 76; polishing/rejuvenating, 74, 120; speaker mount, 35 lifelines: chafing gear, 65; drink holders, 149; rigging fenders on, 50; rigging jib net, 107; securing/tensioning, 67; single-hander's safety lanyard, 173; webbing straps as, 68

lifeline stanchions: fittings for, 66; installing, 61; as solar panel mount, 38; strengthening, 66

lighting, cabin, letting in natural light, 74

lights: anchor, 45; compass, 42; running, electricity for, 131

lines: cam-cleat holder, 101; cutting tools, 90, 91; hangup prevention, 100; position markers, 137; safety lanyard, 173; securing, 90, 97; whipping/seizing ends, 87, 91. *See also* dock lines; heaving line; painter; rigging, running; rope; ropework

litter boxes, 165

locker: closure, 118; cockpit, hatch lock, 175; hanging, oar rack inside, 186; hanging, substitute for, 145; removable, for anchor rode, 52; storage diagram, 176

locks, for lockers, 118. *See also* security

log, social, 177

M

mainsail: canvas cover closures, 108; reefing aids, 109, 110; tie-downs, 105

mainsheet, padeye mount for, 82

man-overboard: fender float, 172; safety lanyard, 173

marlinspike work, sealing line ends, 91

mast: silencing wires, 129; stepping aid (daysailers), 133

mast steps, 93

metal polishes, alternative to, 18

mildew, avoiding, 42, 52

mold, avoiding, 42, 52

monkey fist, softball as, 92

mooring pickup: cut-the-shouting headset, 142; simplified, 141; singlehanded, 138, 141

N

nautical charts. *See* charts

navigation lights, wiring/switches, 42

net bag, for rinsing potatoes, 155

netting, agricultural, for shelf storage, 148

netting, foredeck, 67

netting, nylon: for screens, 33, 61; for scrubbing, 14

nonskid. *See* anti-skid

nuts, locking in place with dimples, 8

nylon, ripstop, repair patch, 108

O

oars: rack for storing, 186; as whisker poles, 113

oil changes, 20-24

outboard engine. *See* engine, outboard

P

paddle, as whisker pole, 113

padeye mount, shock-absorbing, 82

padeyes, eyebolts as alternative to, 24

paint. *See* anti-fouling paint; gelcoat

paintbrushes, stored in freezer, 89

painter, dinghy, 184

pennants: care, 167; halyard tension, 166

pests, 164

PFDs stored as cushions, 175

photos as postcards, 167

pilings, tie-ups at, 48, 135

pipe/tubing, PVC: cutting, 10; uses, 15, 28, 37, 66, 100, 102, 135

Plexiglas: cleaning/polishing, 74, 75, 120; instrument covers, 75; polishing/rejuvenating, 75, 120; status board, 177

polish: for Lexan/Plexiglas, 74, 75, 120; for metal, 18

portlights: Lexan/Plexiglas, rejuvenating, 120; plastic covers, 77; privacy covering, 121

postcards, photo, 167

potatoes, rinsing, 155

preventer, 94; as outboard hoist, 181

propane. *See* stove fuel

propeller, anti-fouling treatments, 87

propeller shaft: cutless bearing removal, 26; packing removal, 27; repacking shaft gland, 27

protecting electrical connections, with fingernail polish, 12

pump, air: for clearing engine intake strainer, 7; for clearing stoppages, 7

pump, bilge, for draining sink, 133

pump, fuel, for bleeding lines, 19

pump, oil-change, 21, 23

pump, pumpout: compressing air, 4; pumpout fitting seal, 6

pumps: impeller installation, 19; spares, 19, 39; winterizing, 31; wiring, 39

PVC pipe. *See* pipe/tubing, PVC

R

radar, T-track mount, 41

radio. *See* headset, transmitter/ receiver; VHF radio

rats, 164

records/boat papers, storing/organizing, 178

reefing aids: cringle extension, 109; eliminating sail stop, 110; for roller-furling jib, 101

refueling, diesel, 19

rigging, running: line hangers, 90; mount for mainsheet padeye, 82

rigging, standing: forestay protection, 30; securing while trailering, 129; shroud cleats, 103; shroud covers, 100; spreader boots, 99; staysail-stay storage, 98

rigging terminals, inspecting, 17

rigging wire, cutting, 104

rodents, 164

roll-damping device, 44

roller-furler: preventing halyard wrap, 101; protecting, 30; reefing aid/line holder, 101

rope, synthetic: cutting tools, 90, 91; whipping/seizing ends, 87, 91. *See also* knots; lines

ropework: securing ends, 91; securing knots, 87; tools for, 91; whippings, 91, 137

Roto-Rooter, replacement for, 7

rudder: emergency steering, 172; leaky rudderpost, 16; repair/securing, 174; towing, for inflatable dinghies, 185

S

safety tape, to protect fingers while sanding, 59

sail battens: securing, 114; storage, 114

sail covers, canvas, securing, 108

sail needles, storage, 108

sails: folding/flaking, 16; forepeak storage divider, 53; reefing aids, 109, 110; resinated, cartopping, 115; tie-downs for flaked mainsail, 105. *See also* headsails; jib; mainsail

sail track: alternative (genoa), 106; for bookshelves, 146; eliminating sail stop, 110

sanding: hull bottom, 59; polishing metal, 18; protecting fingers, while, 59

sanding blocks, 59

scraper, substitute, 88

screens for companionway hatch, 33, 61, 62

seat for helmsman, 79

security: cheap alarm system, 174; dimples to lock any nut in place, 8; hatch bolt, 62; single-key padlocks, 176; single-padlock system, 175

settee, side storage access, 144

sewing needles, storage, 108

shelves: book holder, 146; screen storage extenders, 148

showers: garden sprayer as, 131; water heater for, 122

shrouds: boathook storage, 148; covers, 100; securing while trailering, 129

singlehanding: anchoring, 141; backing into slip, 134, 140; docking, 136, 139; man-overboard safety lanyard, 173; mooring pickup, 138, 141; weighing anchor, 143

sink, galley: draining, 125; drink holder mounted on, 149

slip: backing into, 134, 140; docking tips, 136, 137, 139

small items/parts/fittings: storage, 118, 147, 178

solar panels: mounts for, 38, 86

soldering: alternative to, 11

soldering gun/iron: cleaning, 12; as rope/line cutter, 90

spinnaker: dousing/sock snuffer, 111, 112; easier handling, 112

splicing. *See* ropework

spreaders: bird barrier/deterrent, 55, 56; boots for, 99; rigging flag halyard, 166

stairs, milk-crate, 45. *See also* boarding ladder/steps; step

stanchions. *See* lifeline stanchions

stays: backstay, boathook storage, 148; forestay, protection, 30; forestay, securing aid, 132; securing while trailering, 129; staysail stay, storage, 98 steering: emergency, 172; replacing cables, 15. *See also* auto-pilot; tiller; wheel steering

steering pedestal: winch-handle mount, 81

step: for boarding from dinghy, 179, 182; bucket as, 182; cooler as, 128; milk-crate as, 45. *See also* boarding ladder/steps; mast steps

stern pulpit: anchor stowage, 141; outboard tilting aid, 126; solar-panel mount, 38

storage/stowage, 134; anchor/ground tackle, 48, 40, 52, 53, 54; bimini pole, 162; boathook, 148; books, 146; charts, 169, 170; clothes, 145, 148; in coffee table, 145; computer diskettes, 42; dishes/utensils, 150, 151, 152, 155, 157; dock lines, 80; documents/boat papers, 178; emergency tools, 80; glassware, 149, 150, 155; inflatable dinghy, 186; netting, 148; oars, 186; organization diagram, 176; PFDs, 175; in pocketed bag, 144, 147; sails, 53; under seat, 80; in settee/berth, 144; sewing needles, 108; small items/parts/fittings, 118, 147, 178; tools, 118; vegetables, 156; whisker pole, 133

storage bag: heavy-duty, 121; pocketed, 144, 147

storage box: for charts, 170; for plates/utensils, 151

storage rack, teak trivet for, 152

stove, galley: alcohol, filling, 159, 160; counter/chart table over, 170; gimballed, securing, 158; lighting, 155

stove fuel: alcohol, 159, 160; fuel-gauge alternative, 160; propane, 160, 161; storage/ refilling bottles, 159, 160, 161

stuffing box, repacking flax, 1, 27

sun protection, for instrument panel, 76

swimming-pool chlorinating tablets, to make chlorine bleach, 2

T

tables: anti-skid for objects on, 120, 123; chart, 168, 169, 170; cockpit/cocktail, 69, 70, 71, 72, 169; coffee, as storage bin, 145; saloon, 71

tape: vinyl, removing, 14, 60; safety, to protect fingers while sanding, 59

tarp: as storage bag, 121; tie-downs for, 1, 29, 30

terminal fittings, inspecting, 17

through-hulls: mounting without drilling, 37; tube for, 36

tides status board, 177

tie-downs: for covers, 1, 29, 30; for flaked mainsail, 105

tie-ups, at pilings, 135. *See also* dock lines

tiller: for autopilot, 43; cockpit table accommodating, 70, 72; cover for, 84; extension, 64; lock, 63; remote, 143; tamer, 65

tools: color-coded, 20, 178; emergency, 80; organizing/ storage, 20, 80, 118, 178

topping lift: adjustable controls, 95, 96, 97; as outboard hoist, 181

towels, drying, 167

towing dinghy, 184, 185

trailers, boat, tongue extensions for, 130

trailersailing, 33, 126 - 133

transducers: mounting, 37; removing, 36

transmission fluid, topping off, 27

transom slap, quieting, 163

tubing, ABS plastic, uses, 16

turnbuckles, holding with clevis rings, 90

U

utensils, storage, 151, 152

UV protection, for instrument panel, 76

V

varnish: drip-proof can, 89; removal, 88; storing brushes, 89; tough-ups, 88

vegetables, storage, 156

vent, Charlie Noble (stovepipe), foul-weather cap for, 81

vent, cowl, restrainer for, 81

VHF radio: cause of compass error, 36; frequency info, 177; holder, 41; mini-speaker, 36; speaker mount, 35

W

washers, copper, cleaning, 24

water, drinking/fresh: charcoal filters, 153; city water pressure, 123; for coffee, 154; dispenser for ice-cold, 153; filters, 3; rain catchers, 162; from thawed ice, 154; treatment, 2, 3, 153
water heater, 122
water jet, improvised, 4
water lines, winterizing, 31, 32
water pump indicator light, 39
weather status board, 177

weighing anchor. *See* anchor, weighing
wheel steering, cockpit table for, 69
whisker pole: paddle/oar as, 113; storage, 133
winch: as lazaret lid holder, 78; mount for handle, 81
windows: cleaning, 14; rejuvenating Lexan/Plexiglass, 120
windscoop, instant, 85

wine glasses, storage, 150
winterizing: engine, 32; pumps, 31; water lines, 31
wire rope, cutting, 104
wires: snaking, 39; wire-nut connectors, 11, 12
wire ties, declawing, 11
wrench: alternative, 22; color-coding, 20, 33; socket organizer, 33, 118